# CHRISTIAN PARENTING IN TODAY'S WORLD

## A Common Sense Guide for Raising Children In Today's Contemporary Society

By

## David E. Miller, Ph.D., FICPP
## Psychologist

**Xulon**
PRESS

*Christian Parenting In Today's World*
by David E. Miller, Ph.D.

Printed in the United States of America

ISBN 1-59781-914-X

www.xulonpress.com

# Disclaimer

Other than personal examples of Dr. Miller and his own children, the names of patients and some descriptions of their characteristics and symptoms have been slightly altered to protect their confidentiality and privacy.

# Dedication

This book is dedicated to several people who played significant roles in motivating and encouraging me to write it. Perhaps of the most significant are my own children—Scott Alan Miller and Lori Ann (Miller) Hicks. Both grew into beautiful young adults who are now parents to our beautiful grandchildren—Kate Elizabeth, Anna Marie, and Camden Thaddeus—who continuously bring many hours of happiness and joy during this next phase of our lives. Despite the typical mistakes we made as parents, Scott and Lori chose to endorse the values they were taught and saw modeled in our home. Now as grandparents, we serve to support them in their parenting roles and are often blessed to observe traditions that have been passed down from generations before. As Christian parents, Scott and his wife, Cara, and Lori and her husband, Adam, seriously consider the multitude of threats that our contemporary society poses as inconsistent with the traditional Christian values they desire their children learn. As they seek to model the values they want their children to follow, our role as grandparents serve to reinforce and support this extremely important teaching. Many thanks are due my godly parents, Rev. L.B. and Ruth Miller, who first parented me; their example of the values they wished for me to learn was most instrumental in what I have come to believe as important values and have practiced in my own parenting roles. My wife, Joy, who consistently upholds me and my patients in prayer; her constant encouragement and support of my ministry to hurting people provides energy to persevere on those discouraging days that every psychologist in private practice will often face. Without doubt, the countless hundreds of Christian parents who have worked with me in family therapy as they have searched for answers have demonstrated the need for such a project as this self-help resource book. Finally, this book is dedicated to future generations of parents who will search for ways to raise their children in Christian homes while living in a worldly society that chooses to ignore, minimize, or otherwise compromise traditional Christian values or be subtly misled by the contemporary thinking of this era.

# Table of Contents

**Chapter 1**

# Is Christian Parenting Even Possible In Today's World?

꙳

*Show me your ways, O Lord, teach me your paths;*
*guide me in your truth and teach me, for you are God my savior,*
*and my hope is in you all day long.*
*Psalm 25:4-5*

In today's fast-paced world, many Christian parents ask whether there is sufficient time to do an adequate job of raising their children. Within the Christian home, parenting responsibilities should rank extremely high among other tasks and be considered an important obligation, a privilege, and a great opportunity to raise children in the sight of God. However, many parents struggle to manage their time and priorities in ways that minimize adverse effects on child rearing. Others feel guilty for not having spent enough time on what they feel is such an important role as their children develop through childhood.

Even if we temporarily disregard the extra effort required of Christian parents, parenting is one of the most difficult roles in adulthood. It is both time-consuming and exhausting, constantly draining available energy levels despite its rewards. At times, parents may feel their parenting tasks are thankless, having few benefits or rewards. At other times, perhaps too infrequently, parents receive a glimmer of appreciation for all the hard work exerted on behalf of their children.

Parenting quite often becomes secondary to other things that demand one's full attention, such as earning a livelihood. In addition to the 40 to 50 hours weekly that most jobs require, there are over-time hours that one is expected to share with co-workers and spend on extra projects, committee meetings, and planning seminars or conferences. Such activities are necessary to advancing in a career and all seem legitimate, yet these obligations compete for a parent's limited time and energy.

Aside from work commitments, school, community and church involvement as well as other activities take their toll on parents. Organizing child care, making preschool arrangements, attending parent-teacher conferences, supporting little league sports and music lessons, and other extracurricular activities important to children's development are only a few of the tasks facing most parents today. Life becomes even more complicated when one spouse is completing college-level coursework or some other form of advanced training that is necessary to retain a job or advance in their career.

A vicious cycle develops as parents find themselves with less-than-adequate time and energy to handle the tasks needing their attention. Despite appropriate priorities, the fast pace we maintain and the demanding society in which we live do not allow sufficient time for everything. Also, many people lack the skills to organize and manage their time effectively, resulting in inefficient use of already limited time.

Quite often, friends request a Christian's assistance or ask them to lend a supporting hand. Christians are supposed to be helpful to others—that's what we've learned from early childhood. Although feeling stressed already and perhaps stretched to the maximum, we find it difficult to explain this concern to others. Despite knowing we don't realistically have time for even one more thing in an already stretched schedule, we respond to such pleas, which only lead to further frustration in trying to balance our scheduling chal-lenges. Unfortunately, family or parenting commitments are quite often postponed. It somehow seems easier to explain to the ones we love the most (family) rather than social acquaintances our inability to keep a commitment. It seems that our family members should understand how busy we are and more willingly accept our inability to give them time. Family and marital therapists report that when one becomes overly stressed, he or she often takes it out on or hurts the people they love the most.

Frequently the request for help may even be made by a pastor or other church leader who we feel is God's servant. A pastor's urgent plea may be made in a manner which conveys that we are uniquely talented and have the necessary attributes for the task at hand. It is further reasoned that there is just no one else who can be recruited, for everyone knows there are few willing workers in most congregations. Perhaps that is why many pastors, in desperation, allow themselves to place many more responsibilities with certain people than they are able to balance with family priorities. With continual urging, a parent's position on priorities may weaken, and perhaps before giving further thought or prayer to the matter, a requested task is reluctantly accepted. In this decision-making process, the issues with the most pressure attached seem to rank higher; the old "squeaky wheel gets the grease" phenomenon seems to apply.

Scripture instructs Christians to seek first God's kingdom and His righteousness, and all these things will be given to them (see Matthew 6:33). Some Christians and even perhaps some well-meaning pastors misinterpret this scripture to mean "putting God and church first" rather than "God first" as intended. God does not and never has intended for anyone to put even the church before family. I Timothy 3:5 states, "If anyone does not know how to manage his own family, how can he take care of God's church?" This implies that people can serve God yet lose their families, and that perhaps God's expectation for the Christian is to rank family as a prerequisite for church work, so that a more balanced commitment can be made.

Some parents so diligently serve their church in a multitude of roles that they become exhausted and cannot deal with their family. This over-involvement can be an escape from parental or marital obligations—perhaps even a shirking of responsibility. Over-involvement precludes the ability to deal effectively with one's marriage and family. A large number of Christian families suddenly find themselves in the middle of marital dysfunction, family conflicts, difficulties in parent-child relationships and communication, and a host of other problems that necessitate professional services from a counselor, therapist, or psychologist.

Obviously, some will go to the other extreme and use the need for family time as an excuse to be totally uninvolved and detached from the church or available ministries. This extreme is just as wrong! One must take a balanced approach to time commitments, making time for the essentials. People usually do what they really want to do, and if the church is prioritized as an essential, it will be given a high priority but not at the expense of family.

It is not my purpose to cause parents to feel worse than they already may regarding their parental roles or to place them on unnecessary guilt trips. Even though modern society has contributed heavily to the time-commitment dilemma, the issue has been raised throughout history. Philosophers have referred to this problem as early as in Socrates' time, as illustrated by the following excerpt from one of his early writings:

> *If I could climb the highest place in Athens, I would lift my voice and proclaim...Fellow citizens, why do ye turn and scrape every stone to gather wealth, and take so little care of your children to whom one day you must relinquish it all? (Socrates)*

The Christian parent must seek insight from Scripture. In Matthew 18, Jesus refers to children as greatest in the kingdom of heaven (see vs. 1-4). The chapter relates the occasion when Jesus' disciples came to Him, asking which one of them would be the greatest in the His kingdom. Not only did Jesus answer their question, but He demonstrated through his analogy that children are very important creatures, not to be minimized, ignored, or forgotten. Rather than present adults as models for children, Christ stated that adults should take notice of and model themselves after children. He went on to demonstrate His feelings regarding children by saying "And whoever welcomes a little child like this in my name welcomes me" (see vs. 5). This exhortation of Christ to His disciples further warns that it would be better for a man to have a large millstone tied around his neck and be drowned in a deep sea as to being found guilty of misleading a child (see vs. 6). This analogy very concisely demonstrates the importance of children and the responsibility that parents have toward them.

Another important implication is found in Matthew 6:33, which reads, "But seek first His Kingdom and His righteousness, and all these things will be given to you as well." In Matthew 6:34, parents are reminded not to worry about tomorrow since tomorrow will worry about itself, and there being enough trouble in a day that one should not give rise to additional ones. So often, we worry about the implications of our time constraints but do little to change our patterns of behavior. This scripture exhorts Christians to place their many tasks and limited time in God's hands and ask for His divine help in ordering them. We must look carefully at our priorities and perhaps eliminate some otherwise worthy activities that deprive our children of the loving companionship that is so essential to their growth. In John 15:5, we are reminded that even if our priorities are worked out in our minds, we still need God. It is only through Him that we can be fruitful in our endeavors. "I am the vine; you are the branches. If a man remains in me and I in him, he will bear much fruit; apart from me you can do nothing."

Not only is Christian parenting a value upheld by Scripture, but to fail in this very important calling has some serious ramifications. First of all, most parents recognize very early that they have become their child's most significant persons or "super heroes." Parents rank alongside the most favorite cartoon or storybook characters. This is one of the reasons parents enjoy their little tikes so much. Affirmation from young children gives many rewards and much satisfaction to parents despite the other challenges and responsibilities that characterize the parenting role. Although parents recognize that they don't have all the answers and are not the smartest or strongest people in the world, they enjoy being made to feel that way by a son's or daughter's early belief system. Parents, therefore, have a very important responsibility—to provide gentle guidance to young lives and minds. Because parents have a very significant influence in a child's development, they must be conscientious in living out their parental roles.

One very important theory supported by a large number of psychologists and child development specialists indicates that children learn about others by first learning about their family and home environment; they then apply this knowledge to others. The following poem by Dorothy Law Nolte, often displayed in the offices of child psychologists and other child development specialists, probably summarizes this theory best:

### Children Learn What They Live

If a child lives with criticism, he learns to condemn.
If a child lives with hostility, he learns to fight.
If a child lives with ridicule, he learns to be shy.
If a child lives with shame, he learns to feel guilty.
If a child lives with tolerance, he learns to be patient.
If a child lives with encouragement, he learns confidence.
If a child lives with praise, he learns to appreciate.
If a child lives with security, he learns to have faith.
If a child lives with approval, he learns to like himself.
If a child lives with acceptance and friends, he learns to
     find love in the world.

If children learn from the behavior observed within their own families how to respond to other people, they must also, perhaps much more importantly, develop an image of God through the image they have of their parents. This concept significantly magnifies the importance of Christian parenting. If a child perceives his parents as unforgiving, he then perceives God as unforgiving. Critical or intolerant parents will no doubt cause their children to attribute similar qualities to God. On the other hand, parents who convey approval, acceptance, security, and fairness contribute positively to their child's developing concept and understanding of God. For this reason, it is most important that parents take a serious look at the attributes they are teaching their children through their modeling.

Some Christians have a perception that since they are Christians they need not worry about the problems commonly associated with inadequate parenting. This is a false assumption and a dangerous oversimplification of God's protection of His children. An increasing number of Christian families are finding themselves in situations requiring professional services. In our contemporary society many forces impact our children's and grandchildren's lives in addition to parenting efforts. This is precisely why parenting and supporting grand-parenting must be such a high priority. Parents compete with some rather powerful influences—television, peers, school, neighborhood, changing values, and especially the explosion of the significant impact of computer technology and the Internet on the moral decay of society—which together monopolize more of the child's time than parental influence and guidance.

Don't become overwhelmed or give up from discouragement! While one cannot perhaps successfully impact the larger system for it is way too powerful; with God's help, parents can significantly affect the small world of their individual family and children. Although Christian parenting has always been a challenge and will remain so for years to come, it is possible to successfully meet this challenge!

# Chapter 2

# The Importance Of A Good Parent-Child Relationship

*Be imitators of God, therefore, as dearly loved children and live a life of love, just as Christ loved us and gave himself up for us as a fragrant offering and sacrifice to God.*
*Ephesians 5:1*

Parents are not automatically ordained with authority when they become parents. They must establish a relationship with their children and become that "significant other" person whom the child learns to love and deeply respect. In an article that has become viewed as a "classic" within the child development field, William Dahms (1) describes authority as a relationship issue. Simply stated, one has no authority over the child unless there is some relationship between that person and the child. As the relationship grows, the level of authority increases.

A quality relationship is one in which the child feels that those in authority are caring, honest, fair, right, reasonable, dependable, openly supportive, and respectful (2). Although Dr. Dahms' article addresses mainly staff members and teachers in schools or other programs for children, much of what he writes is completely relevant regarding parents and the relationship they have with their own children within the home.

Many parents practice methods precisely opposite of what Dr. Dahms advocates for a healthy parent-child relationship. When the relationship is lacking, the adult often resorts to intimidation, threats, fear, and other unhealthy approaches of control. Such methods usually are ineffective in changing a child's behavior. If changes do occur, they are usually superficial and short-lived. How many times have you heard parents say to their children one of the following threatening comments?

"You'll do it because I say so..."
"You'll do it or else..."
"Don't you dare talk to me like that...I'm your father (mother)!"

In my work with parents I often share a story I once heard about a little boy whose mother asked him to be seated, without success. After the boy adamantly refused several times, his mother forcibly sat him in a chair and held him there. She then assertively informed her strong willed son that he would sit there even if she had to hold him in that chair. Even though she had gained physical control of his body, the little boy's will remained, as is always the case, within his own control. In defiance, the little boy looked at his mother and obstinately said, "I may be sitting on the outside, but I'm standing on the inside!" Parents are not always winning the battle, even when it may appear that they have been successful.

How, then, are parents supposed to gain a quality relationship with their children? Our earlier definition of a quality relationship implies that the caregiver or parents must be seen as **caring, honest, fair, right, reasonable, dependable, openly supportive, and respectful.** Parents must behave in a manner that demonstrates these positive qualities to build a good relationship with their children.

# Caring

In examining these qualities further, let's first look at **caring**, which can be demonstrated in a multitude of ways at all age levels. When a child is an infant, parents must care for every aspect of the child's life, from feeding to changing dirty diapers. Adolescents no longer need or want such assistance but need to know that parents support and love them, and that they will be available if necessary. From picking up the crying infant or tending to his or her needs through feeding, comforting, or changing a diaper to conveying to the teenage son or daughter that you are available to talk about the questions they might have about life or the value system you are demanding they follow, the approach parents use during the life cycle must evolve to fit the developmental needs of the child. The manner in which the parent accomplishes this will convey to children the level of care available to them.

We can also communicate care by the way we talk to our children. A caring exchange conveys respect. Adults don't have to talk down to a child or be condescending. The overall manner of handling a child's needs will convey how precious a commodity he or she is. The value parents place on parenting responsibilities is revealed by how they care for their children. Some children quickly perceive how carelessly they are handled by their parents or the other adults in their lives as they observe these persons give more care and focus to a piece of antique furniture, an automobile, a hobby, or something else of value. Involvement in a child's life is a good indication of parental care. From showing interest in homework to playing house, from attending little league games and piano recitals to loaning the family car for that important date—these are all ways to convey interest in their lives and the importance we place on their comfort and happiness.

# Honesty

**Honesty** is necessary for a positive relationship. We should never hide the truth from our children. We can explain things to them much better than any other source they might eventually seek out for answers to their unanswered questions. If something is hidden from children to protect them, they will quite often need explanations at a later time. When things are clarified later, you may also need to handle why the truth was hidden or kept secret to begin with, which may make children feel distrusted or unimportant. Children tend to work out their own rationale regarding family problems or perceived difficulties if explanations are not provided by their parents. Many children perceive marital difficulty within their family before their parents proactively deal with it, often blaming themselves or their behavior for mom and dad's unhappiness. Minor problems may be misinterpreted by children as serious threats to their family and cause feelings of insecurity and anxiety. Children are too perceptive for parents to hide family secrets from them. Of course, one must use common sense and recognize the developmental level of the child in determining to what extent details should be shared. But family secrets seldom ever work and are never right!

## Fairness

**Fairness** is a prerequisite for establishing a positive parent-child relationship. It is sometimes hard for parents to be fair since many perceive themselves as having or needing to have ultimate power over their children. Listening to a child's explanation for misbehavior and giving explanations for discipline is a step in the right direction. Caution should be used in stating to a child that he or she must follow the same rules as a brother or sister; because every child is unique, each may require a different approach to discipline. Rules need to be flexible to accommodate a variety of situations; parents should try to avoid being too rigid with their children. "One size fits all" does not work in child rearing terms. For example, curfews and responsibilities need to be age-appropriate. Obviously, a teenager demonstrating more trustworthy behavior may be legitimately rewarded with fewer boundaries than one who constantly pushes limits and exhibits irresponsible behaviors. A more structured schedule outlining various times for each activity is required for children experiencing school problems to facilitate completion of homework and tutoring while allowing free time for play and recreation.

In most families, parents need to help their children understand financial matters and the need to equitably distribute limited family resources to meet all members' needs. Parents should be careful to prevent younger children from always getting what is left over— either material goods such as hand-me-down clothing or what is left over of the parents' time. A plan that works for many families is scheduling individual time for each child, while at other times arranging activities that include everyone and more "family" focused events. A child needs to perceive that he or she is just as important as other family members who might be older, stronger, smarter, and capable of doing more since they are more mature.

## Being Seen As Right

Parents should strive **to be right** and have the credibility and respect that one acquires for being right. Although we must remain open to admitting when we are wrong, we should strive to model correct behaviors and attitudes for our children. As our children get older, they recognize our limitations and inform us of our inconsistencies. Parents must not panic or reject such feedback, for this is very normal as a child matures. Children simply recognize their parents' limitations as they strive to develop their own competencies as individuals.

Perhaps the best way to reveal the perception that one is right is to live rightly! The most powerful way to communicate our sense of right and wrong is by how we live (3). As already described above, honesty and caring seem pretty important in conveying fairness. Obviously, being reasonable in the expectations we place on our children as well as being willing to listen to their concerns will help them see we are attempting to be fair. As parents, we should avoid preaching honesty to our children if we model dishonesty by cheating on our income tax or driving away from a parked car we have just backed into without notifying the owner. Our actions speak louder than words in situations like these; such actions teach children our true values and demonstrate a lack of integrity rather than what we wish for them to see modeled.

# Being Reasonable

**Being reasonable** is much like being fair. The best method to demonstrate this quality is to eliminate any perception of its opposite — rigidity. Rules, regulations, requests, or instructions are not reasonable just because parents have made them. Parents should try to avoid explaining a rule by the explanation "because I say so." Children deserve to have explanations. While we will need to avoid falling into the trap of answering every "why" raised by the "strong-willed" and resistant child, we should try to explain the rationale for our decisions or discipline. This process of explaining why the rule is needed and how it can help to better decision making or avoid problems is educational; it will help the child understand and learn values. Although this process takes time and effort, it is essential for child-rearing practices.

# Dependability

The next important means of building a relationship with one's child is **to be dependable.** Dependability goes further than just providing for the child's needs consistently. Parents need to prioritize spending quality time with their children and be conscientious in fulfilling this commitment. If our children can't depend on us as their parents, who can they depend on? We should never make promises we can't keep—this only weakens the child's view of our dependability. As dependable parents, we need to be seen as people who can predict when our child will need help and offer our support. The most dependable people I know are my best friends. While careful to remain in the parental role, perhaps showing the dependability of a best friend to your child will ensure this quality.

# Being Supportive And Respectful

**Being supportive and respectful** starts within the home and is then applied to the extended family and other people. Children learn to respect their parents because they see the respect they have for each other and other people outside the family. Children also learn to trust parents because they see their parents demonstrate trustworthiness with others. Parents should look for opportunities to convey respect and support as well as model their support for each other. Comments such as "Let's see how your dad feels about this" or "Let's discuss it with your mother..." tend to reinforce this quality. Of course, we must be genuine in our efforts. It is very difficult to fool our children; they perceive our attitudes and motives despite our attempts to hide them.

# Ingredients Of Effective Parenting

Several years ago while attending an open house at our daughter's school, I received a handout entitled "Five Ingredients for Effective Parenting." These ingredients are closely related to building an appropriate parent-child relationship:

1. *Demonstrate mutual respect.*
   Limit yelling, lecturing, hitting, sarcasm, doing
   things for children they can do for themselves,
   double standards, and negative talk.

2. *Take time for fun.*
   The quantity of time is less important than
   quality of time; spend time each day on things
   both you and your children can enjoy doing.

3. *Use encouragement.*
   Avoid praising the child—praise his or her efforts,
   for such tends to build a sense of adequacy.

4. *Communicate love.*
   This should be done through verbal and nonverbal
   means.

5. *Listen to what the child is not saying.*
   Tune in to the message behind the signal.

# Problems Are Opportunities

Another important issue very closely associated to the parent-child relationship is the parents' attitude. In chapter 1, we tried to illustrate the privilege God has given us as parents in raising our children. Additionally, parenting is described as a process that requires much time, energy, and well planned efforts if parents end that era in their lives feeling success. The attitude of the parent has a lot to do with how much "work" it becomes. A concept I frequently reference in my work with parents is that **problems are opportunities.** Any time a behavior problem erupts, a parent should be semi-enthusiastic, since it becomes an opportunity—both for the parent to teach a value and for the child to learn that value. Such a situation is usually a good learning experience since it springs from real life. Of course, "semi-enthusiasm" does not mean that as Dad catches a lamp that has been overturned in a fight between his children that he leaps for joy and exclaims, "Oh, just what I've been waiting for all day...another opportunity to teach my children proper social skills!" Obviously not! He frantically jumps in to break up the fight and tries to save the lamp in the process. His response is quite likely more human than described above, and he might even be a little angry at his under-socialized offspring, as he concludes in his own mind that surely they take after their mother's side of the family.

If parents can approach a problem with a positive attitude, they can minimize negative effects and reach a solution more easily. Problems are a normal part of life. Edmund Cooke once said, "Trouble is what you make it." Depending upon what we make it, a problem can be devastating or growth enhancing. There is little we can do to prevent some problems from occurring. It is our attitude that allows a problem to remain a problem or makes it an opportunity for growth. **We must approach problems in a proactive rather than reactive manner.** Adopting a calm attitude helps to restore calm. This also reduces any tendency to react negatively and damage the relationships that we are working to develop and maintain.

Our daughter-in-law recently told us of such a parenting challenge involving our two precious granddaughters—Kate Elizabeth (2 ½) and Anna Marie (1). The two girls were playing quietly in their bedroom while both dad and mom were accomplishing other needed household tasks; as they had been extremely quiet for a while, their mother thought she should check on them only to find that they had gotten into the diaper rash treatment and proceeded to give each other a full body treatment as well as generously providing their toys, linens, carpet, walls, and clothing an ample supply of the Vaseline based compound. Tempted to over-react and yell at them for their misbehavior, she quickly realized that they did not know they had done wrong; the expression on their faces and their greeting to mom suggested they anticipated she would be proud of them rather than upset. Realizing this to be the case and that this misbehavior was not an act of defiance or rebellion, the approach she chose was to consider it a learning opportunity and after several baths and hair shampoos later, she chose to take them to the park and spend a few minutes which helped everyone "debrief" and "refuel." Later that night at bedtime, the 2 ½ year old daughter pointed to the wall and said to her mother, "that's a boo boo, mommy." Her mother agreed with her and then lovingly instructed her that we never are to put things on the walls or carpet. This is a beautiful example of approaching what could be considered a major problem and catastrophe with a much more productive attitude of seeing this situation as a potential for learning and teaching.

Parents do need to convey optimism in their parenting efforts. If parents try to increase understanding of their child's behavior, carefully listen to what their children say through words and actions, and concentrate on building a positive parent-child relationship, they will increase their chances for successfully maintaining a positive attitude. Perhaps the most important way to maintain a positive approach with children is to believe in them as individuals. With proper parenting and guidance, I believe all kids are born to win! Unfortunately, many of them have been conditioned to lose (4). This conditioning process begins and ends with a child doubting himself or herself, which is usually the result of careless interactions with the significant adults in that child's life.

## Chapter 3

# Developing Good Communication With Your Child

*Do not let any unwholesome talk come out of your mouths, but only what is helpful for building others up according to their needs, that it may benefit those who listen.*
*Ephesians 4:29*

Thousands of articles, papers, and books have been written on the subject of communication. The manner in which we communicate determines to a large extent just how effective we are at problem solving. When communication channels break down, problem-solving efforts usually cease. This is true with all kinds of interpersonal interaction, including communication between spouses within a marriage, employer-employee relationships, management-union negotiations, and parent-child relationships. In this chapter, we will focus on communication between parent and child, identify styles of interactions that are more effective in solving problems, and target stumbling blocks to effective communication and problem solving.

In *Parent Effectiveness Training,* Thomas Gordon refers to twelve ways in which people communicate a majority of the time. Some of these are not only ineffective but cause further problems for both the person sending the message and the listener, who may hear a distorted message. Others are less problematic; however, none of these twelve methods should become the predominant mode for parent-child communications. A summary of these methods with examples of each follow (1):

## 12 Typical Methods Of Parent-Child Communications

1.  *Ordering, Directing, or Commanding: Telling the child to do something; giving an order or a command*
    *Examples:*
    "I don't care what other parents say; you have to do the yard work...it's your chore!"
    "Don't talk to your mother like that!"
    "Now you go back up there and play with Ginny and Joyce!"
    "Stop complaining..."
    "You will do it because I say so..."

2.  *Warning, Admonishing, Threatening: Telling the child what   consequences will occur if he or she does something*
    *Examples:*
    "If you do that, you'll be sorry!"
    "One more statement like that and you'll leave the room!"
    "You'd better not do that if you know what's good for you!"
    "I would suggest you think about your answer before you give it!"
    "Remember that all our choices have consequences... have you considered what this choice could bring?"

3. *Exhorting, Moralizing, Preaching: Telling the child what he or she ought to do*
*Examples:*
"You shouldn't act like that..."
"You ought to...you should..."
"You must always respect your elders."
"Your decision to participate in that event is wrong... you should be ashamed to have even considered it."

4. *Advising, Giving Solutions or Suggestions: Telling the child how to solve a problem, giving advice or suggestions; providing answers or solutions*
*Examples:*
"Why don't you ask both Ginny and Joyce to play down here?"
"Just wait a couple of years before deciding on college."
"I suggest you talk to your teachers about that."
"Go make friends with some others girls."

5. *Lecturing, Teaching, Giving Logical Arguments: Trying to influence the child with facts, counter-arguments, logic, information, or your own opinions*
*Examples:*
"College can be the most wonderful experience you'll ever have."
"Children must learn how to get along with each other."
"Let's look at the facts about college graduates."
"If kids learn to take responsibility around the house, they'll grow up to be responsible adults."
"Look at it this way—your mother needs help around the house."
"When I was your age, I had twice as much to do as you."

6. ***Judging, Criticizing, Disagreeing, Blaming: Making a negative judgment or evaluation of the child***
*Examples:*
"You're not thinking clearly."
"That's an immature point of view."
"You're very wrong about that."
"I couldn't disagree with you more!"
"I can't believe you could even consider such a thing."

7. ***Praising, Agreeing: Offering a positive evaluation or judgment, agreeing***
*Examples:*
"Well, I think you're pretty."
"You have the ability to do well."
"I think you're right!"
"I agree with you..."

8. ***Name-Calling, Ridiculing, Shaming: Making the child feel foolish, putting the child into a category, shaming him or her***
*Examples:*
"You're a spoiled brat."
"Look here, Mr. Smarty..."
"You're acting like a wild animal!"
"Okay, little baby...here's your pacifier, do you wish for me to change your diaper also?"

9. ***Interpreting, Analyzing, Diagnosing: Telling children what their motives are or analyzing why they are doing or saying something; communicating that you have them figured out or diagnosed***
*Examples:*
"You're just jealous of Ginny."
"You're saying that to bug me..."
"You really don't believe that at all."
"You feel that way because you're not doing well in school."

10. *Reassuring, Sympathizing, Consoling, Supporting:*
    *Trying to make the child feel better, talking him out*
    *of his feelings, trying to make his feelings go away,*
    *denying the strength of his feelings*
*Examples:*
    "You'll feel different tomorrow."
    "All kids go through this sometime."
    "Don't worry; things will work out."
    "You could be an excellent student, with your
    potential."
    "I used to think that too."
    "I know; school can be pretty boring sometimes."
    "You usually get along with other kids very well."

11. *Probing, Questioning, Interrogating: Trying to find*
    *reasons, motives, causes; searching for more informa-*
    *tion to help solve the problem*
*Examples:*
    "When did you start feeling this way?"
    "Why do you suppose you hate school?"
    "Do the kids ever tell you why they don't want to play
    with you?"
    "How many other kids have you talked to about the
    work they have to do as chores?"
    "Who put that idea into your head?"
    "What will you do if you don't go to college?"

12. *Withdrawing, Distracting, Humoring, Diverting:*
    *Trying to get the child away from the problem; with-*
    *drawing from the problem yourself; distracting the*
    *child, kidding him out of it, pushing the problem aside*
*Examples:*
    "Just forget about it..."
    "Let's not talk about it at the dinner table."
    "Come on—let's talk about something more pleasant."
    "How's it going with our basketball team?"

"Why don't you just try burning the school building down since you hate school so much?"
"We've been through all this before."

Although many of the above examples can be effective communication tools at times, Gordon refers to them as "the typical twelve," quite often leading to ineffective communication. This is not to imply they are always bad or never to be used, for there are times that "questioning" to gain further information or "sympathizing" with someone might indeed be appropriate and helpful. "Praising" can be an excellent tool to use with children, for it greatly facilitates building self-esteem. However, if the predominant style of communicating takes on these forms to the exclusion of listening, one can expect to be misunderstood much of the time.

A good number of parents use ordering, preaching, advising, and judging predominantly. However, if they are asked about why they are so negative with their children, they will deny utilizing those styles and rename their communication by such names as "teaching," advising,", and "interpreting" since these latter styles represent qualities of good parenting. No one would question that a good parent teaches, advises, and interprets for their children.

If this is the case, why then are these methods considered inadequate parent to child communication techniques? Dr. Gordon indicates that about 99 out of 100 parents participating in Parent Effectiveness Training classes use ineffective methods of communication with their children. What most parents say to children often does nothing to resolve the problem and instead may worsen the conflict or disagreement. While some interactions cause a child to resist a parent's influence by refusing to change his or her behavior, other interactions make the child feel "dumb" and insulted. Still other interactions make children feel guilty, tear down self-esteem, and cause them to defend themselves vigorously or provoke them to attack parents in a "get-you-back" fashion. Some of us make the mistake of sending a "solution message" to the child; we convey to them what we feel they should do. As parents, we take over by calling the shots and maintaining control. We do this by utilizing one of the four styles described below (3):

# Sending Solution Messages To Our Children

### 1.  *Ordering, Directing, or Commanding:*
"Go find something to play with so you can stop bothering
    me."
"Stop wrinkling the paper."
"Put those pots and pans away."
"Clean up that mess you and your sister made."


### 2.  *Warning, Admonishing, or Threatening:*
"If you don't stop, I'll ground you…"
"Mother will get angry if you don't get out from under my
    feet."
"If you don't get out there and put that kitchen back the
    way it was, you're going to be sorry!"

### 3.  *Exhorting, Preaching, or Moralizing:*
"Don't ever interrupt a person when he's talking."
"Please play someplace else…you are in my way!"
"You shouldn't play when Mother is in a hurry."
"Always clean up after yourself…cleanliness is next to
    Godliness!"

### 4.  *Advising, Giving Suggestions or Solutions:*
"Why don't you go outside and play?"
"Let me suggest something else for you to do."
"Can't you put each thing away after you use it?"


Parents would never talk to another adult the way they quite
often talk to their children. For example, if a friend comes over to
our home and happens to place his foot on the rung of our new
dining room chair, we would never say what most of us say to our
children (4):

"Get your feet off my chair this minute!"
"You should never put your feet on somebody's new chair."

"If you know what's good for you, you'll take your feet off my chair this very minute!"

"I suggest you do not ever put your foot on my chair again, if you know what's good for you!"

While some parents send solution messages, other parents send "put-down" messages. Everyone knows the discomfort that comes after having received a put-down message from another person. Such messages convey blame, judgment, ridicule, criticism, or shame. According to Gordon, put-down messages fall into one of the following categories (5):

## Put-Down Messages Sent To Children

1. *Judging, Criticizing, or Blaming*
*Examples:*
    "You ought to know better."
    "You are being very thoughtless."
    "You are being totally disrespectful!"
    "You are the most inconsiderate child I know…"
    "You'll be the death of me yet!"

2. *Name-Calling, Ridiculing, or Shaming*
    *Examples:*
    "You're a spoiled brat."
    "All right, Mister Busybody…"
    "Do you like being a self-centered person?"
    "Shame on you…you should know better…you didn't learn that from us!"
    "Why did God bless me with two hyper kids?"

3. *Interpreting, Diagnosing, or Psychoanalyzing*
*Examples:*
    "You just want to get some attention."
    "You're trying to get me upset…aren't you?"
    "You just love to see how far you can go before I get mad."
    "You always want to play exactly where I'm working."

"Did you take your medicine this morning or did you forget?"

### 4. *Teaching or Instructing*
**Examples:**
"It's not good manners to interrupt someone."
"Other people take notice of children who obey and respect their parents."
"How would you like it if I did that to you?"
"Why don't you be good for a change and see what happens."
"Do unto others..."
"We don't leave our dishes or other food items in the family room."

All of these "put-down" statements, which depreciate the child as a person and attack his or her self-esteem, cause feelings of inadequacy and resistance on the child's part. When children feel attacked or put-down by another person, they respond by resisting further or attempting to defend themselves from what they see as unfair interactions from that person. Although other significant persons to the child—family member, babysitter, grandparent, or teacher—can participate in this negative process; unfortunately, it is primarily the parental figure that is responsible for the bulk of communication with their children. "These are the ways that parents, day after day, contribute to the destruction of their children's ego or self-esteem. Like drops of water falling on a rock, these daily messages gradually, imperceptibly leave a destructive effect on children (6)."

As already indicated above, there are probably times when each one of the styles making up this list can be very appropriate and necessary. However, each style of communication in this list is potentially hazardous if used out of the appropriate context. Potential misunderstanding or misperception is increased when we adopt these forms of communication as predominant styles. Communication can be viewed much like a two-way street where traffic goes in both directions. Good communication will have action from and to both the "receiver" and the "sender." All interactions must include both the sender and the receiver or there is no communication.

## Good Communication Involves 2 Directions

| *Message Sender* | *Message Receiver* |

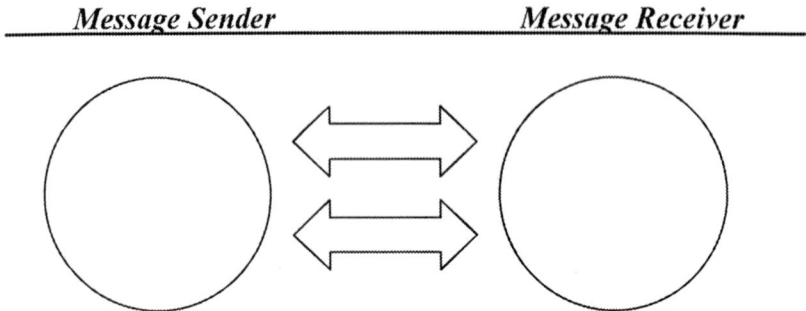

Unless the receiver hears the message being sent by the sender, communication does not occur. If the message received is different than the one intended to be sent, then communication does not occur. In order for communication to be successful, it requires some effort on both parts—the sender and the receiver.

Sometimes a receiver only takes in what he or she would like to hear. This phenomenon is referred to as "selective hearing." The following illustrates this type of communication.

# Selective Hearing

**Selective Hearing**

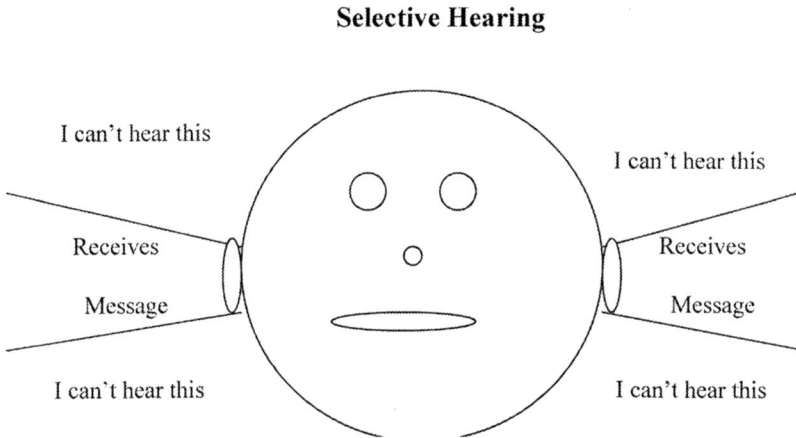

"Selective hearing" prevents us from really listening to others. While this can be extremely frustrating to the parent when a child is exhibiting it because they would prefer to ignore the request or admonition, many parents are guilty of this type of hearing when it comes to their children. Children quickly learn the science of selective hearing through adult modeling. Some children can look at their parents with deep concentration and still not hear the truths imparted. Although the message may have been clearly and concisely delivered, leaving no doubt in the parent's mind as to its meaning, that message wasn't received by the child as intended. If a transmission hasn't been properly received, then communication has not occurred.

# Encoding & Decoding Messages

Another block to communication involves the phenomenon known as "encoding" and "decoding" that is a part of most messages exchanged between two people. Our human nature prevents us from communicating without emotions attached to each concept we wish to share with another person—whether it be with a son or daughter, a spouse, a neighbor, employer, or the waitress attending our table at the local restaurant. To communicate with merely factual information would seem unusual and appear almost like the non-human figure known as Spock in the once popular television show known as Star Trek. Spock experienced no emotions since he was a non-human being; his communication consisted only as factual information without any attached emotion or feeling. Since we are emotional beings, the majority of our communication contains an emotional element.

Communication generally involves the "sender" encoding (or adding the element of emotions or feelings) the message that is being sent; the "receiver" then must go through the process of interpreting or decoding (reducing or separating the message from the emotions or feelings attached) the sent message to insure accuracy of the message. We seldom speak entirely factual with each other; our messages are usually coated with emotions and feelings which increase the possibility of misinterpretation by the receiver of that message. The listener must decode a message to discover its intended meaning. This process of "decoding" whereby we learn to decode messages with more accuracy is what Dr. Gordon termed ACTIVE LISTENING. We will focus more of our attention to active listening in the next chapter.

Consider a boy coming home after school. As he comes through the door he says, "Hi Mom, what's for dinner?" His mother knows that he has probably not taken a sudden interest in nutrition or the evening menu, so long as it excludes such things as asparagus, broccoli, green beans, and peas. His real concern is how soon dinner will be available because he's hungry. Good mothers, as in this example, are usually automatic in their intuitive understanding of their child. After greeting her son, she offers him a cookie or another snack to tide him over until dinner. The following schematic diagram illustrates this basic concept of decoding and encoding messages (7).

# Encoded and Decoded Message

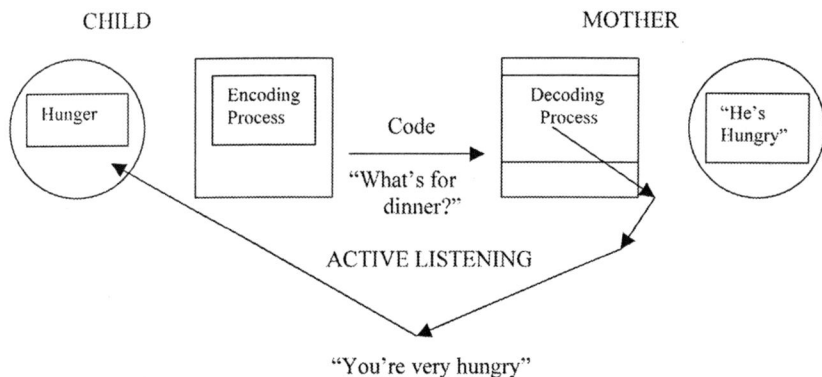

CHILD                                                MOTHER

Hunger     Encoding Process     Code     Decoding Process     "He's Hungry"

"What's for dinner?"

ACTIVE LISTENING

"You're very hungry"

Although this process may seem quite cumbersome to the already busy schedule that most parents keep, it actually can become fairly simple with practice. Like any other skill that we master, the more practice we have, the more competent we become in our communication efforts. Communication is not as much an "art" or "talent" as it is a skill. Therefore, we can learn good communication with practice.

# Chapter 4

# Communicating To Help Solve Problems

*My dear brothers, take note of this: Everyone should be quick to listen, slow to speak, and slow to become angry, for man's anger does not bring about the righteous life that God desires.*
*James 1:19*

If our usual methods of communication are not effective means of communicating with our children, what should we do? Dr. Gordon suggests the process of decoding a message through **active listening**. In active listening, one concentrates on decoding to truly hear the intended message. Gordon maintains that parents can help keep youngsters or adults talking and further clarifying their message through the use of **"door openers."**

Here are a few examples of simple door openers (1):

## Examples Of Door Openers

"I see…"              "Really…"
"Oh."                 "You don't say…"
"Mm hmmm…"            "No fooling."
"How about that…"     "You did, huh?'
"Interesting…!"        "Is that so?"

Other door openers are more specific in their invitation to give more information:

"Tell me about it…"
"I'd like to hear about that…"
"Tell me more."
"I'd be interesting in your point of view."
"Would you like to talk about it?"
"Let's discuss it."
"Let's hear what you have to say."
"Tell me the whole story…"
"Shoot—I'm listening."
"Sounds like you've got something to say about this."
"This seems like something important to you."

These invitations to provide more information encourage the sender to keep talking and help to minimize interference that occurs when the receiver interjects his or her own feelings and thoughts. Door openers convey acceptance and respect, confirming that a child has a right to express how he or she feels, that his or her opinion is valued, and that the listener genuinely cares and is interested in the child.

When children or adults perceive that someone really cares about what they are saying, they know that they are valued. Several years ago, Art Linkletter hosted a program during which he interviewed children before a television audience. He achieved real success in getting children to relate to him simply by using door openers and allowing them to feel he was a truly interested listener. Although I was only a child at the time of seeing this program on television, I was amazed by this man's ability to get kids to say things I knew their parents had probably warned them not to tell anyone outside the family. I can remember thinking that if I had said such things in public, especially on television, I would surely be in trouble. After bending or stooping down to get on the child's eye level, Linkletter would talk to the child with the same respect he would convey for the President of the United States, giving his undivided attention. The results were phenomenal! The playhouse show was very successful for Linkletter; a similar attempt was taken up later by Bill Cosby, and like its forerunner, the show brought much popularity for the comedian's career. Despite strong parental admonitions prior to the show, the powerful active listening practiced by Art Linkletter and later Bill Cosby, paved the way to produce completely open and honest communication from these children who had been selected to appear on the show.

Active listening is a remarkable way to involve the sender with the receiver. Let's return to the schematic diagram used to explain an encoded message.

## Encoded Message: Active Listening

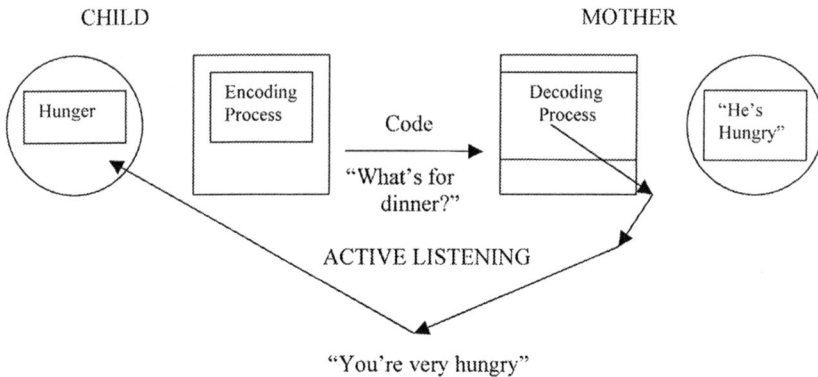

CHILD                              MOTHER

Hunger | Encoding Process | Code  → | Decoding Process | "He's Hungry"

"What's for dinner?"

ACTIVE LISTENING

"You're very hungry"

The receiver becomes active by trying to understand what the sender is feeling or what his message really means. To verify his perception, the receiver puts what he heard into his own words and feeds it back to the sender to validate the message. A few examples taken from *Parent Effectiveness Training* will help to illustrate this point (2).

1.

    Parent:                "You sure feel bad about that—you don't like it when he does that."

    Child:                "That's right."

2. Child:   "I don't have anyone to play with since Sally went on vacation with her family. I just don't know what to do for fun without her."

 Parent:  "You miss having Sally to play with, and you're wondering what you might do to have some fun."

 Child:   "Yeah. Wish I could think of something."

3. Child:   "Boy, do I have a lousy teacher this year. I don't like him. He's an old grouch."

 Parent:  "Sounds like you are really disappointed with your teacher."

 Child:   "I sure am."

4. Child:   "Dad, guess what? I made the basketball team."

 Parent:  "You're really feeling great about that."

 Child:   "Am I ever!"

5. Child:   "Dad, when you were a boy what did you like in a girl? What made you really like a girl?"

 Parent:  "Sounds like you're wondering what you need to get boys to like you, is that right?"

 Child:   "Yeah. They don't seem to like me, and I don't know why."

Notice that the receiver is careful to decode the message without judging or evaluating it. At first, this style of interaction seems strange to those of us who usually communicate in other ways. However, with continual practice, it will seem more natural. If successfully done, active listening can promote a warm parent-child relationship, facilitate problem-solving, and help the child become more receptive to his or her parents' thoughts and ideas.

## Active Listening For Problem Solving

Active listening can often help us in problem solving, but it will not exempt parents from having problems, perhaps better referred to as "challenges," with their youngsters. Let's turn our attention now to **the issue of problem-solving**. First and foremost is to understand when a problem is a problem and to determine who should own or be responsible for the problem. Parents often err in allowing problems that should be the responsibility of their child to become theirs, thus preventing the child from assuming responsibility and changing problem-causing behaviors.

Before we can understand problem ownership, a few basic concepts related to acceptability of behaviors must be addressed. Let's turn again to Gordon's *Parent Effectiveness Training* for a better understanding of these concepts. Problem behaviors can be illustrated by the following schematic (3):

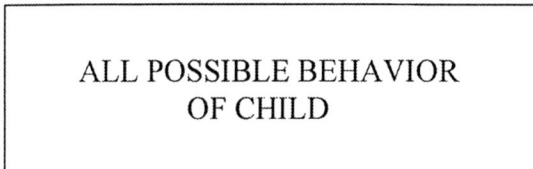

```
┌─────────────────────────────────────┐
│                                      │
│         ALL POSSIBLE BEHAVIOR        │
│              OF CHILD                │
│                                      │
│                                      │
└─────────────────────────────────────┘
```

If a child's life is represented by the box above, then all of that child's behaviors fall inside that structure. Some behaviors are acceptable to parents (okay behaviors), while other behaviors are not (not okay behaviors). In the next illustration, a dotted line separates okay and not okay behaviors. The boundary is dotted because it moves depending on the situation.

# Acceptability of Behaviors

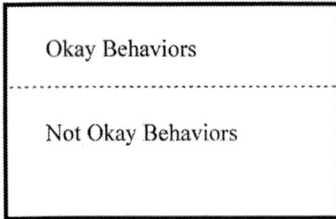

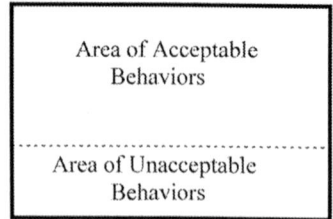

| Okay Behaviors |
| --- |
| Not Okay Behaviors |

| Area of Acceptable Behaviors |
| --- |
| Area of Unacceptable Behaviors |

To demonstrate how a behavior's acceptability can change depending on the situation, let's examine the behavior of **screaming or yelling loudly.**

**At Football Game**

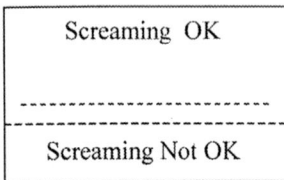

| Screaming  OK |
| --- |
| Screaming Not OK |

**At Church**

| Screaming Not OK |
| --- |
| Screaming OK |

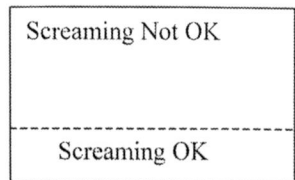

**At Scene of Accident**

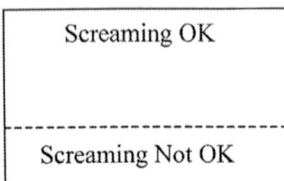

| Screaming OK |
| --- |
| Screaming Not OK |

**At Dinner**

| Screaming Not OK |
| --- |
| Screaming OK |

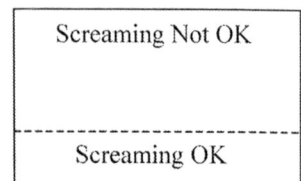

Also, some parents have different standards or levels of tolerance than others. Some are overly accepting or permissive while others are less accepting and more restrictive.

**Overly Accepting or Permissive Parent**    **Less Accepting or Restrictive Parent**

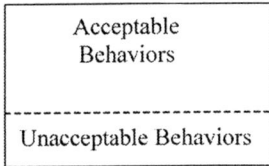

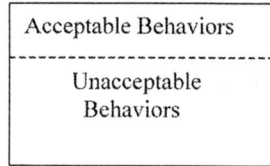

| Acceptable Behaviors |
| --- |
| Unacceptable Behaviors |

| Acceptable Behaviors |
| --- |
| Unacceptable Behaviors |

Both extremes of parenting styles can be problematic. The overly accepting or permissive parent is somewhat neglectful in setting expectations and teaching children societal standards, the difference between right and wrong, and other Christian values. These are children who frequently misbehave in public and in a quite manipulative manner can get their parents to conform to their wishes to avoid embarrassment for the parent. We have all seen examples of this parenting style at the grocery store when the person in front of us has a young obnoxious child that insists on getting a candy bar at the grocery while mom is checking out. Although she initially says "no" to his request, as he escalates his requests to an emotional and whiney demand, she gives in to calm his expression of unacceptable behavior and avoid feeling embarrassed as other people begin observing this drama.

On the other hand, the less accepting parent risks being seen as rigid, unemotional, uncaring, and dictatorial; this style of parenting lays the foundation for a poor parent-child relationship. This type of parenting allows the child no self-expression and the child often responds to the parent much like a new recruit responds to the drill sergeant during boot camp. Although responding for fear of severe consequences, the child quickly learns to resent the parent and within time will begin plotting ways to secretly defy the rules and parental admonitions. Obviously, parents must formulate positions that take into account the age of the child and normal expectations of behavior for that particular developmental age group.

The boundary lines in the acceptable-unacceptable box are also dotted, implying that they too move as the situation demands. Parents are likely to be more accepting of their children when they feel energetic and healthy and are content with themselves. Parents who experience low self-esteem or are angry, hostile, frustrated, stressed, disappointed, depressed, anxious, or tired are usually less accepting of even developmentally normal behaviors of their children.

While occasional problems can arise from "OK" behaviors if the parent is unable to be tolerable and patient with the child's learning to accept limit setting, they usually stem from "NOT OK" behaviors. Discovering who is responsible for the problem quite often reveals what, if anything, one can do to resolve it. For example, if the child owns the problem, parents must insist that the child take responsibility for solving it. If the parent owns it partially, the parent can take responsibility for solving only that portion that involves him or her. The important principle here is that the owner of the problem must assume responsibility for solving the problem. No one else should solve the problem without the owner sanctioning that resolution. A further schematic diagram illustrates problem ownership (4):

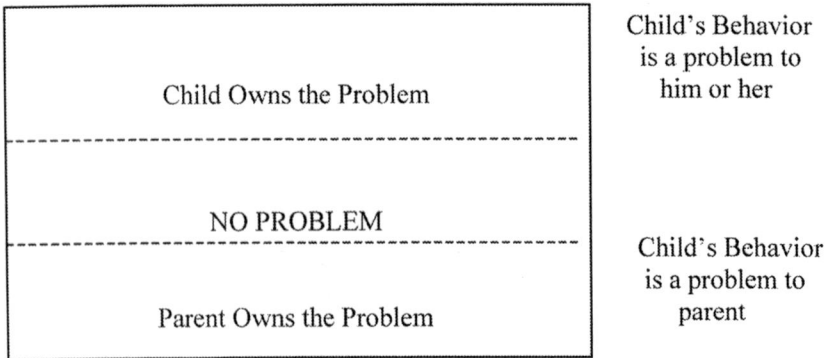

## Problem Ownership

| | |
|---|---|
| Child Owns the Problem | Child's Behavior is a problem to him or her |
| NO PROBLEM | |
| Parent Owns the Problem | Child's Behavior is a problem to parent |

When the child owns a problem, parents should graciously encourage their child to utilize his or her inner resources to solve the problem. This does not imply that parents can't show concern or offer help; parents can always facilitate the resolution of a child's problems. However, the parent should avoid taking over, which excuses the child from responsibility. Many parents make the mistake of taking full responsibility for the problem by dictating a solution. To do this robs children of the important learning experience that struggling to solve a problem provides; it also insults the child's ability by conveying that the parent doesn't believe they can solve problems on their own. Furthermore, if a parent always jumps in to solve their child's problems, they foster dependence rather than independence and the ability to make good decisions in the future.

Active listening, which was discussed in the last chapter on communication, can greatly enhance the effectiveness parents have as helping agents, which is probably much different that the assistance parents typically give to their children. The following excerpt illustrates a typical parent-child problem –solving situation (5).

## Parent-Child Problem Solving Dialogue

**Jason:** "Tommy won't play with me today. He won't ever do what I want him to do!"

**Mother:** "Well, why don't you offer to do what he wants to do? You've got to learn to get along with your friends." (advising or moralizing)

**Jason:** "I don't like to do the things he wants to do, and besides, I don't want to get along with that dope."

**Mother:** "Well, go find someone else to play with then if you're going to be a spoil sport." (offering solution, name-calling)

**Jason:** "He's the spoil sport, not me. And there isn't anyone else to play with."

**Mother:** "You're just upset because you're tired. You'll feel better about this tomorrow." (interpreting, reassuring)

**Jason:** "I'm not tired, and I won't feel different tomorrow. You just don't understand how much I hate the little squirt!"

**Mother:** "Now stop talking like that! If I ever hear you talk about one of your friends like that again, you'll be sorry." (ordering, threatening)

**Jason:** (walking away, sulking) "I hate this neighborhood. I wish we would move."

The same scenario with active listening follows (6):

**Jason:** "Tommy won't play with me today. He won't ever do what I want to do."

**Mother:** "You're kind of angry with Tommy." (active listening)

**Jason:** "That's right. But if I don't have him for a friend, I won't have anyone to play with!"

**Mother:** "You would hate to be left with no one." (active listening)

**Jason:** "I never used to be mad at him, but that's when he was always willing to do what I wanted to do. He won't let me boss him around anymore."

**Mother:** "Tommy isn't so easy to influence now." (active listening)

**Jason:** "He sure isn't. He seems more grown up...he's not such a baby now. He's more fun, though!"

**Mother:** "You really like him better this way." (active listening)

**Jason:** "Yeah. But it's hard to stop bossing him...I'm so use to it. Maybe we wouldn't fight so much if I let him have his way once in a while. Do you think that might work, mom?"

**Mother:** "You're thinking that if you might give in occasionally, it might help." (active listening)

**Jason:** "Yeah, maybe it would. I'll try it."

As Jason finishes this conversation with his mother, he might express his thanks for helping him reach this resolution in his thinking. As he does this, either verbally or non-verbally, it is a wonderful opportunity for his mother to reinforce and validate his problem solving skills. Perhaps that scenario would go something like this:

**Jason:** "Yeah, maybe it would...I'll try this. Thanks mom!"

**Mother:** "Well, you are certainly welcome my son, but I think you pretty much worked that problem out on your own...I just listened while you came up with a solution to the problem. You're really pretty smart when it comes to working problems like this out...your dad and I are very proud of you, Jason!"

Active listening requires us to stay in tune with our own feelings and not allow them to creep into our communication. While parents should convey acceptance to their children, many parents communicate the opposite by sending what communication experts call **"you-messages"** to their children. Examples of such messages that will produce feelings of rejection rather than acceptance follow (7):

# You Messages

"You stop that"
"You shouldn't do that..."

"Don't you ever..."
"If you don't stop that, then..."
"You are naughty!"
"You're acting like a baby."
"You want attention."
"Why don't you be good?"
"You should know better..."

A further example utilizing the following schematic diagram helps to understand the difference between **"you-messages"** and **"I-messages"** (8):

## "You" Message

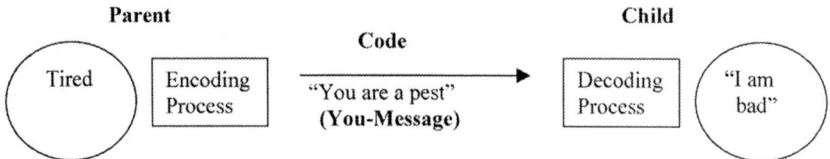

## "I" Message

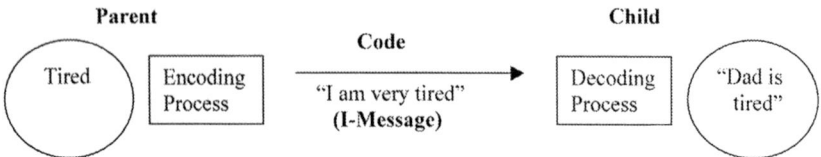

Rather than sending a "you-message," communication experts promote what is called an "I-message." The sender of an I-message concentrates on his or her personal feelings without judging or criticizing someone else. One will often feel judged or attacked by a you-message, but that risk is far less with an I-message, which conveys how the sender feels. Such a message usually stimulates further discussion, rather than shutting it down. A "you-message"

usually closes the door to further discussion; such a message will have several negative results such as making the recipient defensive, feel attacked or misunderstood, angry, and can cause the recipient to withdraw.

Adults typically send "you-messages" to children since they are viewed as immature and perhaps not sophisticated enough to be affected by this form of communication. However, sending predominantly you-messages to our children connote disrespect, appears condescending to the recipient, and lays the groundwork for later power struggles that no one wins. The following examples are examples of I-messages should help to clarify this concept (8):

## Examples of "I" Messages

"I cannot rest when someone is crawling on my lap."
"I don't feel like playing when I'm tired."
"I can't cook when I have to walk around pots and pans on the
    floor."
"I'm worried about getting dinner ready on time."
"I sure get discouraged when I see my clean kitchen dirty
    again."

Lastly, and probably the most important, a simple problem-solving framework will help parents resolve problems with their children and teach them a logical problem-solving method to use in future situations. Children may need a visual model that is presented in steps that help break down the process and lead to a successful solution. If used consistently in an open, caring home atmosphere based on love and mutual respect, a problem-solving framework can reduce parent-child conflicts. The following is an example of a model that many parents have found helpful:

## Steps to Successful Problem Solving

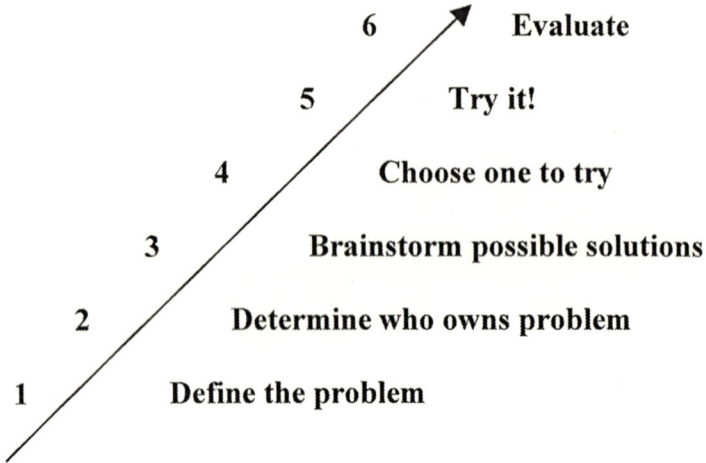

6    Evaluate

5    Try it!

4    Choose one to try

3    Brainstorm possible solutions

2    Determine who owns problem

1    Define the problem

Parents may also find that reference to the **LADDER OF SUCCESS** can be helpful in encouraging their children to strive for success in problem solving. The difference between "I won't" and I did" is a large one. Children should be challenged to be successful at 70 percent or above. Reference to such visual aids can help children understand the importance of the effort they need to exert in accomplishing their goals or better understanding the expectations their parents have for them.

# Ladder of Success

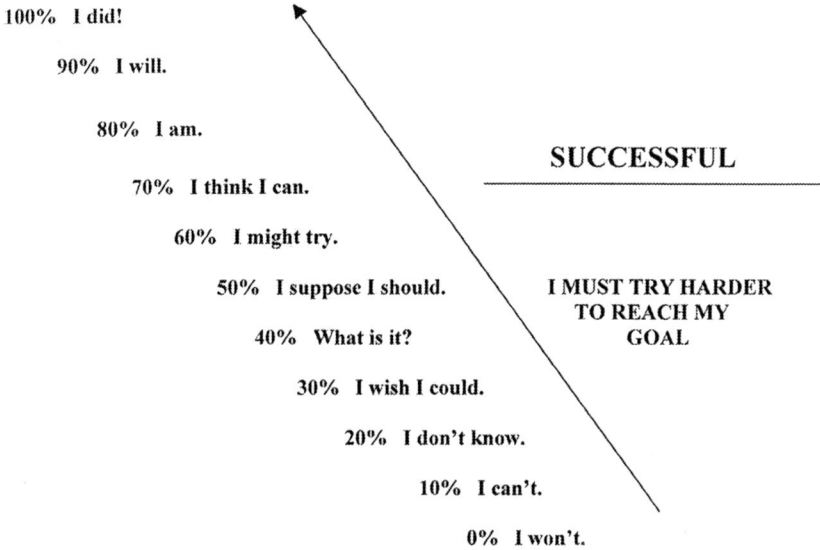

100%  I did!

   90%  I will.

      80%  I am.

         70%  I think I can.

            60%  I might try.

               50%  I suppose I should.

              40%  What is it?

                 30%  I wish I could.

                   20%  I don't know.

                     10%  I can't.

                       0%  I won't.

## SUCCESSFUL

I MUST TRY HARDER
TO REACH MY
GOAL

# Chapter 5

# Understanding Your Children

✣

*Then you will understand the fear of the Lord and find the knowledge of God. Proverbs 2:5*

Parents may make the mistake of trying to understand a child's behavior rather than the child. Art Linkletter told a story about a little girl who lived in an orphanage. Apparently, when she was assigned to the facility, very little background information was provided to the staff. Within only the first few days, her behavior greatly concerned staff members; she did not play with peers or communicate with anyone—neither peers nor adults. Despite the many attempts to communicate with her, all efforts seemed fruitless. There didn't seem to be any explanation for the child's behavior, which continued to perplex the staff because she was so different from other children they had served.

Finally, in desperation, a special staff meeting was called, which included all the staff who had worked with the girl since her admission to the facility. This group of professionals, which included her teacher, house parents, counselor, and, of course, the psychologist, met to review her case. After discussion from all members of this team of professionals, they came to the conclusion that this child seemed secretive and manipulative; her behavior did not appear to be normal. Following this deliberation, it was decided to place the child on 24-hour-a-day observation in an effort to find some clue that might help them further understand what seemed to be significant problems.

Several days passed, but still no answers became apparent to her observers. Then one day the girl was playing on the playground somewhat apart from the other children. She looked around the playground as if to see whether anyone was watching her, slipped away from the group, and proceeded toward a grove of trees behind the building. Cautiously, the teacher on duty watched her every movement from around the corner of the building. Consistent with the staff's assumptions about the girl's secrecy and manipulation, the teacher speculated that the child had perhaps stolen something from one of her peers or off the teacher's desk and was attempting to hide it. Looking about again to ensure no one was watching, the little girl reached into her pocket and then carefully placed what she had removed on the lower limb of a tree. She then hurried back to join the rest of the children; it appeared that none of the others had noticed her absence from the group.

The teacher hurried toward the tree, thinking of the pride she would feel when her administrator and the other staff learned of her discovery which could lead to solving this puzzling case. The teacher quickly retrieved the object from the tree—a small piece of paper that had been carefully folded several times. Hurriedly opening it, the teacher realized that it was a note written in the little girl's own handwriting. The note simply read, "Whoever finds this, I love you!"

The underlying cause of the little girl's behavior was much different than the adults observing her wanted to believe. Although desperately desiring for someone to love her, this child had no understanding of how to meet her need. Once her behavior was better understood, what was previously judged as misbehavior was redefined as meaningful behavior. A child's behavior is often the only means they have for expressing themselves; perhaps we need to diagnose or judge less and seek to understand. We often misunderstand our children's behavior because we fail to listen. One child expressed it like this:

## *Listen*

*When I ask you to listen to me and you start giving advice,
  you have not done what I asked.*
*When I ask you to listen to me and you begin to tell me why I
  shouldn't feel this way, you are trampling on my feelings.*
*When I ask you to listen to me and you feel you have to do
  something to solve my problems, you have failed me,
  strange as that may seem.*
*Perhaps that's why prayer works for some people.*
*Because God is mute and He doesn't offer advice or try to
  fix things, He just listens and trusts you to work it out for
  yourself.*
*So please, just listen and hear me.*
*And if you want to talk, wait a few minutes for your turn and
  I promise*
*I'll listen to you.*

### *(Author Unknown)*

Far too often we try to understand the behavior we observe, become frustrated with our lack of understanding, and many times give up rather than concentrate our attention on the child and our relationship. By understanding the child first, we can then better understand the meaning of his or her behavior.

Further understanding comes with knowledge! Most parents are so overwhelmed by the misbehaviors they fear will embarrass them in public that they take little time to compare the behavior with age-appropriate norms. Some behaviors should be expected and will, with time, take care of themselves. However, many of us cannot stand the thought of allowing our children to be anything but angelic in the eyes of others, especially our friends and family. We place so much pressure on them to comply with our wishes that we destroy their trust, becoming dictators rather than facilitators in the growing-up process. Sometimes we expect too much—other times not enough! Goals should be commensurate with the capacity of a given age or developmental stage to ensure children's success. Many parents get frustrated when their children fail, but the expectations may be too much or too high. Success should be built into reasonable goals that challenge the child but are still achievable.

The following is an abbreviated list of normal developmental expectations adapted from works that many child development experts still consider relevant today--Gessell Institute of Human Development. This list can be used by parents to help them better understand their children and age-appropriate behaviors. These descriptions of behavior represent average developmental levels based on norms for the age group. Individual differences are to be expected. The following charts identify expected behaviors for preschool children aged two to five years followed by descriptions of normal behaviors from age six through late adolescence (1). This information for preschool children will be presented in four categories of information:

> **Social**: Personal behavior in relation to other children, adults and groups
> **Physical**: Motor characteristics, routine needs, specific skills
> **Mental**: Language, curiosity, investigation, exploration, and questions
> **Emotional**: Feelings of affection, anger, fear, jealousy, anxiety and sympathy

## 2 year olds

### Social

Runs-about; self-centered; negativism—"no" is a frequent response; enjoys solitary play; contacts playmates or siblings physically; conforms domestically; stands and watches other children play; something of a "dawdler"

### Physical

Runs more than walks; may appear to have tastes of an acrobat; likes to fill and empty cans or containers with sand or water; likes to knock down blocks; grasps spoon between thumb and index finger; either a messy or spotless eater; goes upstairs with both feet on each step; helps dress self; can ride kiddi-car

## Mental

Motor minded; acquires words; chatters happily; short attention span; likes to investigate and touch things with hands or mouth; frequently asks "where" or "what;" knows night and day; names objects; listens to stories with pictures over and over again

## Emotional

Selfish and self-centered; lacks control; cries easily; frequent outbursts of anger common; shows affection spontaneously; cries when he/she fails to accomplish a goal; shy with strangers

# 3 year olds

## Social

Daring, desires to please; socializes his/her behavior; likes parallel types of play; resents being helped and will have a "do it myself attitude;" cooperative play sketchy; can be bargained with; will have interest in other persons; girls seem ahead of boys

## Physical

Likes active large muscle play; bowel and bladder control established; feeds self with spoon and small fork; can open door and turn faucet on and off; helps to bathe self; can hop on one foot, run, dig, climb, and jump; can ride bike; will help set table

## Mental

Materialistic; converses; interested in color, texture, music and rhythms; frequently asks "why;" asks questions about God, death, sex, etc.; counts two objects; repeats short sentences; tells simple stories of daily happenings; knows name and address

## Emotional

Easily stirred emotionally (temper, fears, excitement); outbursts common but brief; can feel prolonged anxiety; capable of jealousy; apt to be possessive; likes friendly verbal humor; can hold him/herself in anticipation

# 4 year olds

## Social

Finding out important; self-assertive; independent and sociable; forms friendships; longs to play with older children; "bossiness" common; awareness of attitudes and opinion of others

## Physical

More refined and precise gestures; buttons clothes; laces shoes; toilets self; washes hands without help; likes to climb, balance, and jump; goes up and down stairs using alternate feet; can climb a tree and come down by self; fairly independent in eating

## Mental

Imaginative; sophisticated; verbal assertiveness and exaggeration common; tells original story-mixing the truth and fiction; does not like to repeat; knows afternoon from morning and yesterday from tomorrow; enjoys simple folk and fairy tales; can count to 10

## Emotional

Sociable; sophisticated; many fears persist; senses right and wrong; confusion of truth; beginning of pity and feeling "sorry" for others; learning sense of values (right, wrong, good, bad); likes to dramatize

# 5 year olds

## Social

Dependable; self-assurance and conformability; ready for community experience; frequently "shows-off" or appears "silly;" capacity for friendship; protective toward younger playmates or siblings; can respect authority of those who supervise him/her; can be cooperative and self-reliant

## Physical

Controlled; mature sense of balance; dresses self; brushes teeth; combs hair; precision and command of tools; can jig, hop, skip to rhythm changes; laces and ties shoes or skates

# Mental

Concrete thinking; speaks distinctly and with complete sentences; perception of order; form, and detail; some sense of time now possible; realistic; asks for information, enjoys humor; laughs heartily at funny pictures; knows colors; can carry a tune

# Emotional

Reliable; stable; well adjusted; innocent of certain complex emotions; capable of anxiety and unreasonable fears; transfer of affection from mother to father; loves to receive

## Early Childhood Through Adolescence

Six years old through early and late adolescence levels will be broken into a variety of categories that will be relevant for each developmental level.

## Six Year Old

# Tumultuous & Emotional

Very difficult period from 5 ½ to 6 ½...the six year old is very much like the two year old in many ways; violently emotional...loves one minute and hates the next; feelings are extreme and intense; mother is no longer the center of his/her world...**He or She is!;** wants everything first and must be first at everything; must have the most; mothers get blamed for everything regardless of the circumstances; unable to accept criticism, blame, or punishment; he/she has to be right and wants to be praised; has to win; is rigid and not as adaptable with others; has to have things done his/her own way; others must give into him/her; if winning he/she is fine; if not winning, tears and accusations that others are cheating common; will be warm, enthusiastic, eager, and ready for anything when things are going his/her way; tears and tantrums will result when things are not going as desired

# Eating

Perpetual motion and unpredictable; has tremendous appetite with eyes usually bigger than stomach; breakfast usually most difficult meal; may experience nausea at breakfast; intake increases as day goes on; demands sizeable bed time snack and may awaken during the night hungry; not able to sit still at meal times and may seem to be in constant motion

## Sleeping
Beginning to have dreams about death, ghosts, and skeletons; will have good dreams as well; boys generally dream about fires; girls often dream of injury to mother

## Elimination
Mostly responsible but may have to make a last minute dash to bathroom; will become very upset with any accident; boys will be slower to master night time bladder control than girls (bedwetting not unusual at this age)

## Tension Outlets
Generally restless and clumsy; can fall over a piece of string; sitting on edge of chair and falling off common; temper tantrums return; spitting and stuttering common

## Fears
Very fearful especially of noises; fear of ghosts and witches common; fear of someone under his/her bed not unusual; some fear of the elements (fire, water, and thunder); fears sleeping alone or being only one on a floor of the house; fears others will hit him/her; seems brave about big hurts but fears splinters or little cuts; may be fearful of nose drops or swallowing pills

## Sexuality
Strong interest in origin of babies; interested in how baby gets out of mother and if this hurts; some interest in how baby started; increased awareness and interest in sexual differences and will have many questions; mild sex play (playing doctor) and exhibitionism in play and school bathrooms somewhat common

## Parent/Child Relationships

Relationship with mother seems to fall apart; mother becomes primary target for anger and rejection; relationship with father usually much better than ever before; time when father is more effective parent and needs to be involved in child's routines as well as trips to doctors, dentists, school functions, etc.

## Siblings

Bossy; will fight, hurt, and tattle on younger siblings; instigates and likes to see younger siblings punished; refusing to listen to older siblings who may be left to baby sit common

# Seven Year Old

## Mopey and Moody

Seven year old is more withdrawn, calmer, perhaps easier to live with, but will have more complaints; withdraws from conflict and people; likes to be alone; wants his/her own room; more interest in non-participatory activities such as television, radio, reading, electronic or computer games

## Fears

Fears are often stimulated by the news; will have many fears, especially visual (dark, attic, cellar, and shadows); will be fearful of wars, spies, burglars, people hiding; will worry a great deal about being late for school or not being liked by peers

## Sexuality

Wants a baby in the family; knows babies are repeated and that older women don't have them; interest in mother's pregnancy and baby's growth; interest in books about source of babies; generally satisfied with brief and factual explanations

## Parent/Child Relationship

Feels parents do not like him at times; fantasies of rich parents and adoption not uncommon; can be moody with mother and exhibit much sulking; less positive relationship with father than at 6 year old level however, may seem to worship father and confide in him

## Siblings

Quieter, slightly improved relationship with siblings; frequently will compare privileges; will like the role of the older sibling; may demonstrate some teasing

## School

Often cranky and tired; complaints common, worries particularly about unknown teacher; will need personal support; may be more dependent upon the teacher; boys fall in love with teacher and give her presents; may be hard to finish assignments or tasks, sensitive to praise and criticism, doesn't respond quickly and will often detour from requested task

## <u>Eight Year Old</u>

### Vigorous

The eight year old is ready to go out into the world; nothing is too difficult; meets challenges but generally over estimates his/her abilities; energy sometimes followed by failure and tears; may express "I always do it wrong!"

Speedy; busy; new things; friends; dramatizes; needs protection from self-criticism and trying to do too much; interest in both sides of a relationship and it is important to know what other people think; demands closeness, especially from mother; expects more from others; parents can begin to get a hint as to the kind of person this child will become...

### Bedtime

Still may be an issue—many times bedtime is improved with limited use of a radio or music; beginning to resist parental authority and may choose bedtime as the issue

# Dreams
Dreams often are about swimming, flying, movement; scary dreams can usually be traced to TV, books, stories, and parents can help control these by limit setting on such activities prior to bed time...

# Fears
Fewer fears; less worried; less fear of the dark; less fear of school...

# Sexuality
Understands slow growth process; wants to know where baby is and is confused by the role of mother's stomach; information from parents preferred to books; girls are more likely to ask about father's role; interest in sex play is high; dirty jokes and profanity may increase; sex play often occurs if children left unsupervised with nothing to do; sex play needs to be approached calmly and treated as other behaviors requiring parental intervention...

# Parent/Child Relationship
Child haunts mother; wants mother to think the same as he/she does and is sensitive to her approval; wants to meet mother's standards; first deep relationships for the child; less intense relationship with the father and is able to accept father's making mistakes; jealous of mother/father relationship; will respond to and obey father better...

# Siblings
Problems increase; teasing, selfishness; some interest in family background

# School
Eight year old enjoys school; very major need to communicate and to express his/her opinion; especially responsive to praise; generally obeys, however may argue first; immediate rewards help; no longer wants detailed directions (feels it is too babyish)

# <u>Nine Year Old</u>
## Thoughtful and Mysterious

Ready for anything; demands to be extremely independent; friends and peers become more important than family; resists too much "bossing" from parents; looks at adults from interest in what they can do for him/her and not interested in the relationship; adults can't impose themselves on a nine year old; if treated as the mature creature he/she tries to portray, things go pretty well; can be fairly self-reliant and capable

The nine year old can be a worrier; takes things too seriously; can be extremely anxious and may go to pieces over minor things; much worry and complaining—a somewhat neurotic age... Nine is an age of rebellion; passively rebelling and more actively through complaining

Nine year old will complain of tasks being difficult--both at home and school; many complaints of physical discomfort: stomach aches, eyes hurt, etc; although discomfort is real, it is associated with complaint (eyes hurt when he/she has to read, stomach hurts when he/she has to rake the yard, hands hurt when he/she has to practice the piano, has to go the bathroom when he/she has to do dishes or some other chore)

## Eating
Generally no problems; may refuse to eat meats and chicken—particularly fats

## Sleeping
Usually area to challenge parents' authority and may need to negotiate a later bedtime; appeal to his/her maturity (i.e. no stalling or complaining and getting up in the morning without difficulties...)

## Tension Outlets

Physical complaints; stamping feet; playing with buttons on shirt, dress, or coat; drops and breaks things; growling and muttering common; complaints of feeling dizzy...

## Fears

Fears are reasonable; generally concerned with personal failure and his/her inabilities; many fears will focus on school performance

## Sexuality

Most know about menstruation; interest in father's role of reproduction; more appreciation of books on the subject; interested in the differences between sexes—much swapping of sexual information with peers; seeking sexual pictures in books common; beginning of sexual swearing and interest in poems with sexual themes

## Parent/Child Relationship

Suddenly friends are more important than family; many times this is real loss for mother and there is temptation to deal with this through excessive demands and directions; time to reduce unnecessary commands and directives; children competitive regarding parents' occupations and father a bit more important than in the past

## Ten Year Old
### Peaceful

For the ten year old, parent's word is law; all of his/her choices are presented in terms of his parents' sanctions or limits; "yes, Mom says I can..." or "No, my parents won't let me..."

The ten year old obeys easily and naturally and expects to gain status by his/her obedience; not only does he/she obey, but expresses pleasure with his/her family in general; usually nice and friendly to others; is matter-of-fact and straight forward; flexible; doesn't take things too seriously; an age of predictability and comfortable equilibrium; adults receive whole hearted and unreserved acceptance

## Eating
Continues to increase in appetite; 10 year old even dreams of food; not a time to consider diets unless the child is grossly overweight; has not yet made association between food eaten and weight gain

## Sleeping
Usually no problems associated with bed time or sleeping

## Tension Outlets
Same as a nine year old...

## Fears
Many fears (animals, especially snakes and wild animals); fears high places, fires, criminals; beginning to mention things they are not afraid of (dark and being alone)

## Sexuality
Knowledge level and sexual interest similar to nine year old—will begin to tell and have some basic understanding of "dirty jokes..."

## Parent/Child Relationships
Happy and conforming; accepts that parents know best; many will not follow directions immediately—but will comply; high point of father/child relationship; father can do no wrong in child's view

## Eleven To Thirteen

Children vary greatly during this age range; generally they are similar in terms of developmental process; time of great physical and behavioral change which ends with puberty; physiological growth intensifies; increase in hormones; many inner tensions; boys sometimes feel masculinity threatened and may react with aggressive behaviors

Body movements express their attitudes about their bodies; many are disharmonious and gangly; the body is the focus of most attention; deviations from the development of peers causes feelings of inferiority

Friends become more important and help deal with upsets and help them to externalize their feelings...allows closeness to peers, not parents; girls interested in rock stars while boys interested in athletes; an interest in these adult role models or idols, but interest does not include parents

# ADOLESCENCE
## Fourteen to Sixteen

## Social Development

### Family
Overt expression of independence requires acceptance and facilitation; possible conflict over restrictions on driving...may resent limitations imposed

### Peers
Preoccupation with acceptance by social group; intimate and casual heterosexual activity and experimentation common; boys and girls have a few close friends of both sexes; friendships last longer; increase in conflict between peer and adult roles common; independent judgment emerges despite tendency to conformity; girls continue to be more socially adept than boys; primary groups continue to be same sex, but more heterosexual interaction beginning to occur; peer group influences greatly intensified

### School
Plans for investigating career choices; strongly expresses opinions and beliefs which may be contrary to those of school personnel

# Self Development

## Emotions
Competitive peer relationships produce some distrust; daydreaming is common; confides more in friends than in parents; assurance of acceptance and security from parents is still necessary; emotional energy continues to be expanded toward physical change and developing heterosexual relationships; worries about physical appearance, attractiveness and physical development

## Values
Interest in philosophical, ethical, and religious problems; is aware of and verbalizes contradictions in moral code; group beliefs important in influencing values

## Self
Achieving independence from parents; developing socially responsible behavior and achieving new and more mature relationships with age mates of both sexes important

# Thinking/Language Development

## Thinking
Makes fine conceptual distinctions; concerned with the hypothetical, the future and the remote; increased capacity for planning; considers long-range purposes; formulates and tests hypotheses to consider all possible ways a problem can be solved; deals with logical and imaginary solutions; aspirations frequently exceed capabilities; uses abstract rules to solve problems

## Language
Should be able to use language to express and clarify complex concepts

## Physical Development

Adolescent growth spurt at peak for boys, with changes in body proportions, resulting in awkwardness; pubescent stage for boys; secondary sex characteristics continue to develop; early or late physical maturing has less impact on girls than on boys, especially in regard to self concept

## <u>Adolescence</u>
## Seventeen to Nineteen

## Social Development

### Family
Parental advice and support important in transition to adulthood, i.e. career, economic, and marital decisions; may be leaving home for extended period; enjoys freedom, but feels doubts; with more freedom, makes more independent judgments regarding alcohol, drugs, etc...

### Peers
Choice and decisions reflect continuing peer influence; exploring possibilities of becoming more desirable as a mate; group activities provide an outlet for expressing feelings; may be living full time with peers in a college setting; new interpersonal satisfactions and problems common

### School
Has responsibility for decisions to be made in post-high school education

## Self Development

### Emotions
Worries about career choices and other aspects of future; anxious about formulation and continuation of intimate heterosexual relationships; may be experiencing a wholehearted love affair

## Values

Integration of values into a personal philosophy including ethical and moral standards to be used in adult life; is able to make a personal commitment to causes

## Self

Moves toward permanence in job choice, training, education; looking for permanence in intimate relationships; looking for assurance regarding future economic security; may be directly involved in own marital and family life decisions

# Thinking/Language Development

## Thinking

Continues to refine language and thinking abilities; increased life experiences provide more and new opportunities for refinement of previously learned reasoning-thinking skills

## Language

Inadequate language skills may adversely affect job opportunities and limit career choices

# Physical Development

Full physical development for both boys and girls; a majority of both sexes have had physical contact of a sexual nature; both sexes are struggling to learn socially approved outlets for sexual arousal

# Chapter 6

# Parents Must Be A Team!

*Make every effort to keep the unity of the spirit
through the bond of peace.*
*Ephesians 4:3*

Most parents would agree that one important element in a winning football season is teamwork. It has often been said that teamwork is even more important than a good coaching staff. If the team is strong, it can be successful regardless of the coaching. The opposite is also true in that no matter how good the coaching, if the team is weak, it may never see success. The team that doesn't apply good teamwork principles becomes a group without common goals and usually doesn't make it to the play-offs.

Parents must follow the same principles that teams do to be successful in reaching their goals. Successful parenting, even if you apply all the important concepts described in this book, doesn't happen automatically. To maximize the chance for success, both mom and dad must work together and have common goals. There is comfort in difficult times when you have support from a partner or team player. Roles, responsibilities, and necessary commitments can be shared, thus making the often arduous task of parenting more successful and perhaps even more enjoyable. During a crisis, it is always nice to know that you are not facing that little monster or big monster, whatever the case may be, by yourself.

Teamwork is one of the most fundamental concepts of parenting. It's absolutely more important than a set of skills—it's an attitude and a commitment! We can adopt this attitude by attempting to share equally in the responsibilities as well as the joys of parenting. Many a young father passes out his birth announcements and proudly shows his newborn pictures to co-workers and friends, however, then leaves the ongoing tasks of raising that child to his wife. He may show renewed interest during the little league years to take pride in his son's accomplishments but is uninvolved with anything other than sports. All of parenting must be shared, not just selected events or stages. It is easy to parent during the good times. The more difficult challenges are just as important, since successful parenting during these times will help us face future challenges that test our resources and tend to be anything but rewarding experiences.

Perhaps the concept of teamwork can be best understood by breaking the word down as follows:

# TEAMWORK = T E A M

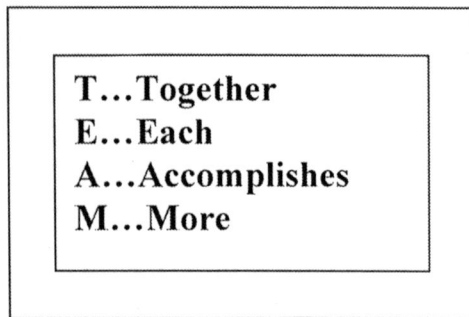

**T...Together**
**E...Each**
**A...Accomplishes**
**M...More**

Teamwork implies that each member of the team is a contributing member. By contributing the skills one possesses, each member strengthens the team. Combined efforts mean more resources and creativity. Parents must support each other in their parenting responsibilities. Rather than be critical of each other, they must give each other support and encouragement. Mutual respect of team members is of utmost importance. Respect not only maintains good team spirit and high morale; it has learning value for children who see their parents modeling cooperation and performing as a team.

If parents truly accept the need for teamwork and work together in rearing their children, there is absolutely no challenge beyond their capabilities. Parents can combine their resources of intelligence, experience, and creativity to deal with just a few years of the child's mischief and manipulation. Parents can always "outfox" their children if they combine their resources. This, of course, implies that problems and the responsibility for solving them are shared by both persons on the team.

In attempting to give parents confidence they can solve any problem their child could create, I will sometimes ask them to add their ages together which gives them the combined years of experience the team possesses. Then I request that they compare that figure with the age of the child. Similarly, I might have them figure their combined years of education and compare it to the grade level or years of experience of the child; this comparison can be somewhat helpful in demonstrating the level of sophistication the parental team has as compared to the child or even a group of siblings that are "ganging up" on the parental team.

Practicing teamwork may not yield perfection, but it brings parents closer to success. No one accomplishes good teamwork overnight. Attaining this skill may take several months or even years. Like any skill, the more parents truly practice it, the better they become. A good coach schedules several practice sessions prior to the game, which helps to increase team members' confidence and level of skills.

## Teamwork: Willingness To Work Together

If teamwork is the answer to good parenting, how does one go about developing it? First of all, teamwork must be understood as a willingness to work together in harmony. **Parents must have a cooperative attitude if they are to be a team.** Team members who play as individuals have a difficult time formulating common goals and working together to accomplish those goals. Yet some parents tend to go about their parenting tasks as if they are doing shift work. Instead of pooling resources, they work independently—much like a "want-to-be" basketball star player who hogs the ball throughout the game rather than implementing the strategies the coach has designed that involve several of the team players. Parents must have a commitment to work together. **They may not always agree on everything, but they must have a commitment to cooperate and compromise so they provide a united front.** It will be virtually impossible for two adults to agree on every issue of parenting for their children. However, there must be willingness to compromise and to blend opinions by consensus into something they both can support. Modeling how differences are resolved, compromises are made, and teamwork is more effective than working as individuals unilaterally, all teach children by parental example.

## Technical & Interpersonal Skills In Teamwork

Teamwork is probably better understood if we break it down into its component parts: technical skills and interpersonal skills. Technical skills involve good parenting techniques, or the how-to methods in parenting. **Being consistent, setting priorities, communicating effectively, implementing good discipline rather than merely punitive measures, and good decision making are all important technical skills.** Technical skills can be learned and refined through practice. **Interpersonal skills include those that facilitate good relationships and getting along with others: acceptance of constructive criticism, willingness to compromise, openness, respect, tolerance of another person's viewpoint, and a positive attitude.**

Inconsistency between parents can cause confusion about expectations and will probably frustrate the child. This frustration can lead to rebellion, withdrawal, or even manipulation by using parent's inconsistency to gain control or advantage. Setting mutually agreed-upon priorities and balancing them with other important activities are important technical skills. For example, participation in sports can be very important in building social skills, however, that participation must be balanced with homework and family activities. If grades fall during a sports season and parents ignore the importance of academics, they are telling their children that sports are more important than education.

Obviously, **balancing priorities also demands another technical skill—time management.** Helping the child manage his or her time in a way that balances priorities is a good lesson that will have greater application as commitments and responsibilities grow. Parents need to practice good decision making and certainly good communication skills that will help to facilitate decision making. Setting priorities will come easier if both parents are able to discuss the important values through good communication. While both parents' participation is important for some things, dividing responsibilities to help balance commitments may prove helpful and make more time for shared family activities.

Aside from making parenting an easier task for parents, teamwork is also important since "teamwork" provides a good model of cooperation for children. Research on how children learn has suggested that most of a child's behavior is acquired by watching other people do the behavior and then imitating it through modeling (1). In regard to modeling, James Dobson says that children "catch" more things than they are taught directly. A good teacher recognizes the importance of providing experiential situations in which students can apply knowledge. Sometimes, seeing a skill demonstrated makes learning that skill much easier. Seeing a principle in action can help a child understand it better.

If you ever want to amuse yourself in a shopping mall, just take a few minutes and observe people. Find a youngster of toddler age and an accompanying parent and observe how the youngster tries to mimic the adult. You'll see the powerful concept of modeling illustrated in real life. As a graduate student several years ago, I would often study at a desk in our family room. My son Scott was about three years of age at the time. He, too, had a small desk placed right beside mine. He consistently watched me study my various psychology textbooks. As I underscored several lines of important information, he would likewise underscore his books with a pencil in exactly the same manner he had seen me do.

## Motivating A Child To Model After Parent

There are certain conditions that motivate a child to model after someone. First of all, the model is usually a "significant other" person for the child. Becoming a significant other for children does not automatically occur because someone becomes their parent. Parents earn this distinction by building the kind of relationship previously described. Research has also confirmed that children model after adults they perceive as being competent and having high status, and who reinforce the child for modeling after them.

Achieving high status with our children is not hard when they are at preschool age, but as time goes on, high status comes only with a growing positive relationship based on love, care, concern, and trust. When we reinforce our children for modeling after us, we are obviously rewarding behavior we wish to have repeated, therefore, strengthening that behavior.

## Children — An Excellent Source Of Feedback

Children are an excellent source of feedback; they may also reflect less-than-positive behaviors they have seen modeled by us. If a child exhibits a behavior modeled by another source that parents do not wish to have repeated, this problem can be easily remedied by offering alternative modeling. As parents, our influence should be greater than other sources if we have become that "significant other" to our children and maintained this important status through our on-going relationship with them. By our attitudes and behavior, we provide children with examples of how to react in similar situations (2).

# Chapter 7

# Understanding Punishment And Discipline

*Discipline your son, and he will give you peace; he will bring delight to your soul. Proverbs 29:17*

Probably more than any other area, parents request help with discipline. The majority of parents want ready-made recipes that are guaranteed to work. Unfortunately, there are no such guarantees. This chapter will address some basic principles of discipline, review the differences between punishment and discipline, and consider the question of corporal punishment, or spanking, which remains quite controversial with many Christian parents. The chapter to follow will build on this discussion of principles by offering specific techniques for effective discipline.

## Positive Relationships

As already emphasized, a prerequisite to good parent-child interactions is a *solid, positive relationship* between the parent and child. Without this relationship, there is no authority, and parents resort to intimidation, threats, fear, and other antagonizing means to force or impose their will upon the child. Most children desire to please parents whom they have come to trust and love.

## Problems Are Opportunities

A principle worth repeating is that *problems are opportunities*. Parents must accept that problems are normal for children and a regular challenge for their parenting skills. If we as parents get overwhelmed by our child's misbehavior, we will hardly be in a frame of mind to use this situation to teach the child. Remember that most of us, even as adults, learn best through experience, quite often through our failures or mistakes. Edmund Cooke once said, "Trouble is what you make it." Some parents make misbehavior a much bigger problem and far more trouble than it really is. By making it a catastrophe, they ruin the potential learning that such a situation affords. Each naturally occurring problem provides parents with opportunities to teach important lessons and values to their children.

## Controlling the Environmental Factors

*Controlling the environment or making planned changes* in environmental conditions can sometimes alter a behavior without saying anything to the child. Many parents create a home environment that is so restrictive and boring that it invites misbehavior. As the old cliché goes, "Idle hands are the devil's workshop." Children often create their own entertainment by manipulating parents, trying to get away with as much as they can, testing their parents' tolerance and limits, and many other less desirable things that antagonize and test the patience of parents. Children need to know what is expected of them and to have a predictable routine (established bedtimes, meal times, homework schedule, curfews, etc.). If this type of structure is absent from the home environment, children tend to test their limits. Through "testing behavior," children are essentially asking for limits to be established. A structured routine or schedule that provides predictability from one day to the next actually provides security to children. All children need a sense of security.

# Power of Touch

Parents who wish to establish a foundation for good discipline should not underestimate the ***power of touch***. Perhaps the following poem by Kathleen Keating summarizes this principle best (2).

# Hugs

**There is no such thing as a bad hug:**
**There are only good hugs and great hugs.**
**Hug someone at least once a day and twice on a rainy day.**
**Hug with a smile; closed eyes are optional.**
**A snuggle is a longish hug.**
**Bedtime hugs help chase away bad dreams.**
**Never hug tomorrow someone you could hug today.**

Much of the child development research supports the need for touch stimulation for both emotional and physical health. Almost everyone enjoys being touched; this is particularly true of children. Touch can relieve pain, reduce depression and anxiety, and sometimes has positive effects on children's language development and level of intelligence. Parents tend to forget that sometimes behavior can be altered simply by touching a child at the right moment. Many times a child may be subconsciously acting out to get the attention that such a touch provides. We need to be "touch people" when it comes to our children. Touch speaks deeply to the soul, conveying care and concern, love and appreciation, in a way that words cannot accomplish.

This phenomenon of touch is important for another reason—through it children can learn the difference between appropriate touching and inappropriate touching. Sexual abuse of children is increasing in our society as with other forms of abuse. Children who come from homes where touching is not practiced might be at greater risk for abuse by others because they have a need for affection that is unmet in their own homes. When faced with the beginning stages of an abuser's approach, the touching quite often seems harmless to a child. Even though the child may have some ambivalence, the need to be touched and his or her difficulty in discerning the difference between a good and bad touch quite often allows a child to accept an abuser's initial efforts. By the time such touching becomes obviously wrong to the child, it may be too late to avoid its harmful effects. The resulting guilt that such abuse leaves with a child, adds to the threats and conditioning to not tell anyone from the offender, and often causes him or her to avoid telling parents or someone that can help stop the abuse from happening.

## Discipline vs. Punishment

Before delving into specific disciplinary techniques, we need to examine the differences between discipline and punishment and to look at corporal punishment. Many parents understand discipline and punishment as equal or synonymous, although they are in fact quite different and in many respects are opposites. Discipline is sometimes used to label what a parent punitively administers to a child and which is actually punishment rather than discipline. Discipline is actually a learning experience that sets behavioral limits and guidelines to help children progress successfully to adulthood. Punishment quite often is used to hurt by causing physical or psychological pain (2).

Of course, the theory underlying punishment is that the child will learn to avoid pain and therefore cease to behave in a manner that could result in such a consequence. Discipline, on the other hand, always contains a learning aspect and focuses on internalizing a value, which then helps the child to cease behaviors inconsistent with the internalized value. Discipline can be a positive experience, but punishment is almost always a negative experience with several less-than-desirable consequences.

Discipline facilitates growth, learning, and a healthy sense of responsibility; punishment, on the other hand, causes children to feel shame and guilt. Punishment attacks the child's self-esteem, but discipline teaches children how to raise self-esteem by taking responsibility for and control of their behavior.

# Purposes of Discipline

The Child Discipline Guidelines for Parents set forth the purposes of discipline as follows (3):

(1) to teach children how to achieve for themselves
(2) to lead children to self-discipline so that they will behave properly without parental or adult guidance
(3) to help children experience pride and pleasure when they do what is right

Thus good parents discipline so that they can facilitate growth of their children toward becoming independent, self-sufficient adults who make responsible decisions. The National Committee for Prevention of Child Abuse (4) characterizes discipline as helping children control and change their behavior, guiding them into adulthood. It enhances a child's self-worth by treating him or her with respect and taking the time required to help a child learn important lessons. Discipline is best taught by example (5). The model we provide as parents is a far more effective teaching tool than anything we verbalize—actions speak louder than words!

Just as discipline tends to build a child's self-esteem, punishment tends to destroy it; additionally, punishment appears to cause other negative emotional responses such as fear, anxiety, hate, resentment, withdrawal, and isolation. Some argue that punishment does work toward a reduction or complete elimination of the negative behavior that precedes it, therefore justifying it as means to an end. However, one must not be too quick to accept punishment as a viable alternative in parenting without first considering its outcomes.

## Some Dangers Associated With Punishment

In a rather dated study, yet still considered relevant today, Krumboltz and Krumboltz (6) report that punishment has some serious dangers: (1) attempted punishment may serve as reinforcement, thereby increasing rather than reducing the undesired behavior, (2) children tend to resist punishment by fighting back, actively escaping, or by withdrawing into passive apathy, and (3) a child tends to avoid the punisher whenever possible. Obviously, these drawbacks can seriously hamper the parent-child relationship which we have already described as one of the most important elements in parenting.

Furthermore, if punishment is upheld, there is no room left for reconciliation. If it is too severe, there is no way to take the punishment back. Finally, even if punishment seems to work, its results will probably be short-lived; the punished child has learned only to avoid a behavior and the subsequent punishment rather than internalize values, understand why such behavior is unacceptable, and then choose more appropriate behaviors. Some children quickly become immune to punishment, making even short-term effectiveness questionable.

## The Controversial Issue of Spanking

If a parent's role in the home is only to inflict punishment, mistakenly viewed as discipline, parents should not be surprised when their child becomes hateful, distant, sullen, and difficult (7). One common means of inflicting punishment is spanking; spanking has all the negative aspects of punishment described above. It can be a violent act that demonstrates using physical force to promote a parent's cause—hardly a social skill parents should be modeling or otherwise teaching their children. It is poor communication in that it is usually imparted in anger, generally offers no explanation, and has many negative ramifications. Spanking, or otherwise referenced as "corporal punishment," does not usually help children internalize any value; it simply causes them to suppress the associated behaviors to avoid such response from the caregivers.

Spanking is also a poor excuse for parental discipline in that it requires little creativity. Many parents who advocate spanking tend to be somewhat lax in taking responsibility for disciplining their children. They choose spanking because it is quick and easy, and it doesn't require much thinking. We have all seen numerous examples of this in the super market or some other public place. We are inconvenienced, perhaps even bothered by a child who is acting out and becoming rather obnoxious to us and others around him. Wondering why his or her parent's level of tolerance is far greater than we would be with our own child if the situation were reversed, we are disgusted to observe how the parent ignores, enables, or even reinforces this behavior.

In such a case as this, it seems as if the parent must feel their little one is "so cute" and wonderful that those of us waiting in the grocery check-out line should appreciate his or her entertainment as we pass the time. Then finally, the child "crosses the line" of the parent and the parent reaches down and smacks the rear end side of the child. The rest of his audience is probably delighted something has finally been done to alter the program we have been forced to watch, but the child is completely caught off guard and usually reacts in surprise—often just escalating the problem further.

What should have happened in such an instance is a variety of interventions that are far more creative and have much more of a teaching value. Since most children enjoy shopping with his or her parent, some rules should be established prior to the trip. If rules are followed, the child could be reinforced by praise, a special treat, and the natural consequence of opportunities for future trips. If the child begins to violate the established rules and doesn't respond to a gentle reminder by the parent, then cutting the trip short or even aborting it midstream and taking the child home would have a greater impact than smacking the child in public. Here the child loses the privilege of shopping with mom or dad since he or she has demonstrated they are not mature enough to participate in such an activity. Since the child desires to accompany his or her parent, mom or dad has the power in getting the child to conform so future trips will be possible.

Smacking the child in public causes embarrassment and directly attacks his or her self-esteem. In reaction to the parent's action, the child usually tries to save face and retaliates, which generally escalates the problem further rather than leading to resolution and a change of behavior. Although it takes far more planning and creativity to handle "shopping trip misbehavior" in this manner, the learning potential is far greater and the problem gets corrected more thoroughly than delaying and procrastinating until the parent can tolerate no more and then smacking the child and threatening further corporal punishment if the problem doesn't cease to occur.

What about Christian parents who advocate physical punishment because they claim it is scriptural? My response is that anyone can quote Scripture to support a practice they wish to justify. The references quoted most often in support of corporal punishment are found in Proverbs:

**Proverbs 13:24**
**He who spares the rod hates his son, but he who loves him is careful to discipline him.**


**Proverbs 22:15**
**Folly is bound up in the heart of a child, but the rod of discipline will drive it far from him.**

**Proverbs 23:13-14**
**Do not withhold discipline from a child; if you punish him with the rod, he will not die. Punish him with the rod and save his soul from death.**

**Proverbs 29:17**
**Discipline your son, and he will give you peace; he will bring delight to your soul.**

The word *correction* or *correct* in the King James Version has been translated as *discipline* in the New International Version. However, in light of our understanding of discipline and punishment, the reference to "beating with a rod" would seem to be punishment rather than discipline.

Those who quote Proverbs as justification for corporal punishment will completely ignore or discount Deuteronomy 13:6-10, which instructs one to stone to death the child who entices anyone to worship another god. Proverbs, by definition, is a book of "wise old sayings." Deuteronomy is one of the books of the Law. Would not a book of the Law carry more weight than a book of wise old sayings?

Yet Proverbs is interpreted literally to support corporal punishment, and Deuteronomy is interpreted figuratively and rejected as not having application in the modern world.

Beyond the selective application of Scripture to justify or rationalize a parent's desire to utilize corporal punishment, one must consider interpretation of scripture as a necessary component in understanding it. Scriptural interpretations are quite often figurative, rather than literal. Understanding modern day application of scripture must take into account the original writings, the context in which it was written, and then very cautiously make application to modern-day. For example, in biblical days, the rod was not just any pole or stick; it was a symbol of miraculous power. In Psalm 23, the rod symbolizes gentleness: "Your rod and your staff, they comfort me" (v.4).

Rather than focusing on the proverbs of Solomon, whose life was characterized by poor values and questionable morals at times, let us turn our attention to the Master himself, who said, "I tell you the truth, unless you change and become like little children, you will never enter the Kingdom of Heaven" (Matthew 18:3). Perhaps it is said best by the Committee to End Violence Against the Next Generation in its publication *The Bible and the Rod (8):*

> To Jesus, not only did the grown-ups not have all the answers, but they may have forgotten things that they knew in youth. Many things fade as we depart from childhood. The power to laugh joyfully, to dream and imagine, to love truly, and form deep relationships, to believe in wonders, and sense the things of the Spirit. In teaching youth our knowledge, instead of "beating the foolishness out of them" we may have something to learn in return.

Christ emphasized the importance of children and their ultimate value to Him. In Mark 10:14, we read "Let the little children to come to me, and do not hinder them, for the kingdom of God belongs to such as these." Christ further warns in Luke 17:2 that it would be better for one to have a millstone hung around his neck and be thrown into the sea than to cause a child to sin. Jesus never used force against or caused pain to human beings or to the beasts of the land, and certainly not to children, whom He presented as models of the innocence necessary to please God. Rather than promoting pain or suffering, Christ represents love as described in I John 4:18, "There is no fear in love...perfect love drives out fear, because fear has to do with punishment...man who fears God is not made perfect in love."

Parents are admonished in Ephesians 6:4, "Do not exasperate your children; instead, bring them up in the training and instruction of the Lord." *Exasperate* means "to make more sharp or severe; aggravate, to embitter or irritate" (9). Of course spanking, a form of punishment, engenders hurt and anger.

Having worked with emotionally disturbed children and their families for the bulk of my career as a Christian Psychologist, I have met hundreds of children who have been physically abused by their parents or caregivers—quite often one of the causes for the resulting emotional disturbance. Such children are angry and hostile, and they fear trusting any adult; their anger precludes the ability to love and trust others.

## Is Corporate Punishment Ever Appropriate?

Is corporate punishment ever appropriate? Perhaps physical punishment might be appropriate if immediate action is required to prevent a child from engaging in a life-threatening behavior, but even then its effectiveness must be weighed against its multiple negative ramifications. For example, if a two-year-old child repeatedly runs into a busy street and the parent has tried unsuccessfully to change this behavior with non-punitive measures, punishment might be necessary—that behavior must be stopped! The two-year-old child has not developed the cognitive skills that allow him or her to understand the reasoning behind a parent's demand not to play in the middle of a busy street. If the behavior is not changed, the child could be severely injured or even face death when being struck by oncoming traffic.

Here, the child can learn that a spanking always follows running into the street and thereby ceases the behavior to avoid the spanking.

However, as soon as the child is old enough to reason in simple cognitive terms, it is important to find alternative means of disciplining the child. Physical punishment should only be used as a last resort, and then only in an emergency situation and short-term as previously described. All other uses of corporal punishment should be seriously questioned and replaced with more creative disciplinary methods in which the goal is internalization of values rather than fear.

John E. Valusek, Ph.D., a psychologist who has studied violence and the effects of punishment on children suggests that the various forms of hitting can cross over into what he refers to as abuse quite easily. The following continuum is an adaptation of his "Yardstick of Violence" (10) and illustrates his thinking on the risks of utilizing corporal punishment.

## Risks of Using Corporal Punishment

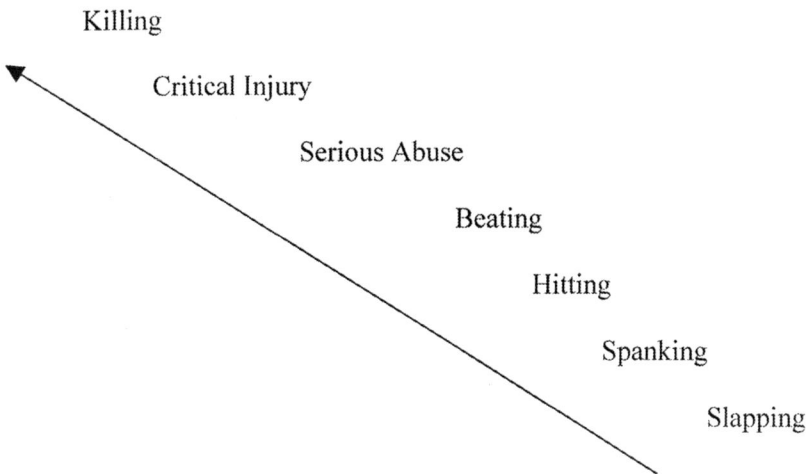

Killing

Critical Injury

Serious Abuse

Beating

Hitting

Spanking

Slapping

While most persons would never progress toward critical injury or killing, some parents have and do. Perhaps the majority of us would stop at spanking, but at what point does spanking reach hitting or beating? Both these forms of punishment would be considered abuse by most agencies designed to protect children such as Child

Protective Services and would carry with such charges penalties for the parents convicted of child abuse.

Dr. Valuseck further illustrates his thinking in the following chart (11):

## Some Forms and Variations of Hitting

| Types of Painful Stroke | Instrument | Usual Label or Description | Effect |
|---|---|---|---|
| 1. Single mild slap<br>2. Repeated mild slaps<br>3. Single forceful slap<br>4. Repeated forceful slaps | Open hand | Slapping Or Spanking | Mild to Moderate Pain |
| 5. Single mild stroke<br>6. Repeated mild strokes<br>7. Single forceful strike<br>8. Repeated forceful strikes | Switch, Stick, Ruler Wooden spoon, Hair Brush Fly swatter, or Rolled Newspaper | Spanking | Mild to Moderate or Severe Pain |
| 9. Single blow<br>10. Repeated blows | Belt, Paddle, Rubber hose, Broom handle or electric cord | Spanking, Hitting, Beating or Abuse | Moderate to Severe Pain |

| 11. Single blow  12. Repeated blows | Closed fist | Hitting, Fighting, Battery, or Abuse | Moderate to Severe Pain |
|---|---|---|---|
| 13. Repeated forceful blows | Fists, belts, boards, kicks or blow by any hand-held or thrown object, instrument or weapon | Hitting, Battery, Or Severe Abuse | Severe Pain: Usually requires Medical Attention |
| 14. Single or repeated blows | Any instrument, means or weapon which causes death to occur | Killing or Murder | Severe Pain to End of Life |

As can be easily seen by looking at the effect of each type of stroke, all forms of hitting cause pain. According to our definitions of punishment and discipline, hitting must be classified as punishment, which then carries with it all the negative ramifications associated with it. Valusek points out that although items 1 through 10 are considered discipline if used by parents or school officials, these same items (as well as 11 and 12) are called hitting or fighting if done by children to other children. In this latter case, good parents would be swift to try to eliminate as fighting is not an acceptable social behavior they want their child or children to exhibit.

Hitting can be justified as "discipline" all the way across the continuum to murder. When does hitting become hurtful? When is it too hard? When does one begin to question the safety of the one being hit? What is being modeled for the child by the parent who chooses to spank the child for misbehavior? What effect does hitting (referenced as "spanking" by most advocates of it) have on the parent-child relationship? All of these questions and others should become important issues to parents who wish to use corporal punishment.

In being interviewed by a reporter of a rather large metropolitan newspaper several years ago for a feature on corporal punishment they were doing, I was asked if spanking is ever appropriate. My response indicated that while I would not adamantly oppose physical discipline in all situations, as a principle I would certainly recommend other more appropriate interventions that had more potential for internalizing values and thus changing behaviors over spanking. I further clarified my position by giving the example of the two-year old child who was choosing to run into the busy street that was referenced earlier in this chapter, carefully pointing out that the two-year old might not respond to any other approach as he or she lacked the cognitive development necessary to understand other forms of discipline and the nature of the behavior made it absolutely necessary to alter it to avoid injury or even death to the child due to the severe danger the behavior involved. The reporter obviously desired to advocate the use of spanking as I was significantly misquoted in the article as stating, "Dr. Miller advocates corporal punishment of children, especially for 2 year olds." Obviously I was disappointed the reporter chose to misquote me to support her own position on the topic.

Spanking is obviously a very emotional issue for most parents; it is quite controversial within the field of child development. Some may choose to utilize spanking as a means of disciplining their children and rationalize that their parents utilized it with them, and they turned out okay. Spanking really needs to be considered in light of its goal and subsequent effectiveness as a disciplinary measure. According to Dr. Valusek, hitting is hitting, no matter how you define it, what you call it, or for what use it may be intended! "People are not for hitting...and children are people, too" (12).

# Chapter 8

# Teaching Right From Wrong With Good Discipline

*Children obey your parents in the Lord, for this is right. Honor your father and mother which is the first commandment.*
*Ephesians 6:1*

If physical punishment is not appropriate, then what is? There are hundreds of substitutes for corporal punishment; it can truly become the last resort and need never be used with most children. I will not attempt to discuss every method, but I will present some of the more common-sense approaches that have been found effective. We will look at eight areas: (1) behavioral approaches, (2) the productive use of anxiety, (3) the Stop…Think…Do…Program, (4) reversal of responsibility, (5) logical and natural consequences, (6) mediation training, (7) power struggles, and (8) additional miscellaneous techniques. The chapter will conclude by providing 36 Positive Approaches To Discipline adapted from Saf Lerman's Parent Awareness Training.

# **Behavioral Approaches**

One could be overwhelmed by all the written material available on behavioral techniques recommended in childrearing. However, the fundamental principle of behavioral psychology is a simple one: *reinforcement through reward.* A *REWARD* is defined as an event or a desirable consequence that immediately follows a behavior, resulting in repetition of the behavior (1). People tend to repeat behaviors that result in positive rewards. Positive reinforcement can take two forms: *social and nonsocial. SOCIAL REINFORCEMENT* includes verbal praise, physical gestures of approval and affection, public ceremonial awards in which a child is recognized publicly for behavior or accomplishment, or maybe simply a smile or approving facial expression from a teacher or caregiver. The following example demonstrates social reinforcement:

## *Examples of Social Reinforcement*

*Praise:*         *"You're doing a good job."*
                     *"That's excellent!"*
*Approval:*     *"You're doing very well."*
                     *"I'm proud of you when you do that."*
*Attention:*    *A pat on the back, a smile, or a "Thank you."*

*Informational*    *"That's correct!"*
*Feedback:*      *"You're following directions well."*

## *Nonsocial Reinforcement*

*Nonsocial Reinforcement* involves a tangible reward rather than social interaction or attention. Nonsocial rewards commonly used to reward behavior include such things as candy, tokens, points, money ($5.00 for each A on the report card), or some other tangible item that is desired by the child. Quite often, points are accumulated by children to be traded for some tangible reward or highly sought-after recreational activity. Both social and nonsocial rewards usually work well to motivate children of all ages, and they work best if used in combination with each other. Very few children will argue with a system that allows them to work toward something they desire, whether it is an inexpensive package of candy or a more expensive video game or trip to an amusement park.

## *Behavior Charts*

*Behavior Charts* such as the ones that follow work well in recording checks or points, which can then be used to reach a goal set by parents or caregivers:

# My Job Daily Checklist

| Daily Chores | Days of the Week (X) | | | | | | |
|---|---|---|---|---|---|---|---|
| | M | T | W | TH | F | S | S |
| Brush My Teeth | | | | | | | |
| Make My Own Bed | | | | | | | |
| Clean My Room | | | | | | | |
| Feed & Water Fluffy (pet dog) | | | | | | | |
| Take Trash Out To Garbage Can | | | | | | | |
| Totals | | | | | | | |

# My Behavior Goal Point System

| My Behavior Goals | Days of the Week | | | | | | |
|---|---|---|---|---|---|---|---|
| | M | T | W | TH | F | S | S |
| I Obeyed My Parents Today | | | | | | | |
| I Followed All Rules At School | | | | | | | |
| I Controlled My Temper Without Outbursts | | | | | | | |
| I Was Kind To My Sister | | | | | | | |
| I Went To Bed Without Delays | | | | | | | |
| I Gave At Least One Compliment To My Family | | | | | | | |
| I Used Stop…Think…Do…to Make Good Decisions & Avoid Temper Outbursts | | | | | | | |
| Totals | | | | | | | |

## *Shaping Of Behaviors*

The concept of **SHAPING** simply means that parents set up reinforcements for successive approximations of the desired behavior, in a step-by-step process until the desired behavior is achieved. For example, for a six or seven-year-old child to clean his own room completely each day before leaving for school might be too overwhelming. However, asking the child to make the bed, hang play clothes on the appropriate closet hook, and place toys in the toy chest are small steps that can be successfully accomplished. Success with smaller steps leads to the long-range goal of leaving the room in a neat, orderly fashion each morning. It is important for parents to refer to developmental norms and appropriate expectations to ensure their small steps are within the range that can be expected of children the age of their son or daughter. Success must be built in so that children feel successful and are motivated to perform these tasks.

## *Response Cost*

The opposite of earning a reward is losing one—*RESPONSE COST*. While children can earn checks for appropriate behaviors, they could lose some for misbehavior. Although not recommended for frequent use, this approach has a learning component; just as an adult recognizes the importance of driving the speed limit after receiving a speeding ticket, a child learns from response cost.

## *Timeout*

A child might also be given a *RESTRICTION or GROUNDING,* during which time he or she is not permitted to earn privileges or participate in normal activities. This form of discipline or grounding is termed *TIME OUT FROM REINFORCEMENT* or *TIME OUT* for short. This is similar to suspension of a privilege because a child demonstrated a lack of responsibility regarding that specific privilege. For example, a parent might choose to ground a teenager from driving the family car for a day or two after being caught driving beyond the speed limit or without regard to traffic safety rules. Another example might involve the elementary aged child grounded from video games since he violated the time limits set by his parents and sneaked to play additional games instead of following bedtime rules.

## *Written Contract*

At times, setting up a *WRITTEN CONTRACT* with a child can have a positive effect in motivating behavioral change. For example, if grades are a problem for Chris, the following contract between Chris and his parents might help to bring about change.

### Contract Between Chris & Parents

*I, <u>Chris</u>, promise to study one hour each night and try to raise my grades by one letter grade during this next grading period. If successful in keeping this promise of studying and raising the letter grades, it is agreed that I will receive a bonus of $20 from my parents and a weekend fishing trip with dad and a friend of my choice.*

*Signed: _____ (Chris)  Date: _____*

*_____ (Dad)     _____ (Mom)*

It is important that the contract conditions be attractive to both parties and stated in simple, understandable terms. The requested change should be easily measured (for example, increase of one letter grade) and aimed at motivating desired changes in behavior.

## Ignoring Certain Behaviors

Sometimes, parents must simply *IGNORE* misbehavior. Parents often focus so much attention on misbehavior that they reinforce it rather than correct it, especially if they unknowingly give more attention to misbehavior than they do positive behavior. Such children often fall into the trap of enjoying their parents' attention, no matter what the reason. As a result, they continue misbehaving simply to get the attention they crave so much.

## Incompatible Responses Or Redirection

Another behavioral approach to discipline that works well is offering an *INCOMPATIBLE RESPONSE* or *REDIRECTING* the child's behavior. While a child is misbehaving, the parent offers another more attractive behavior that is completely incompatible with the behavior he or she is currently exhibiting, thereby forcing the child to make a choice. The more enticing the new behavior is, the better the chances that the child will choose it over the misbehavior. Suppose two siblings are fighting in the family room. Of course, both children have a taste for ice cream cones and would do virtually anything to obtain one. Rather than call attention to the fight, the father announces that he is going out for ice cream and wonders if they cared to join him. The two children will generally stop fighting at least long enough to consider their options; and, the father not only demonstrated wisdom in getting his two children to stop fighting, but also provided an activity whereby cooperation is optimized through this family activity.

## *Positive Practice*

One of my favorite behavioral interventions and one that has shown significant success in getting children to change their behavior is called ***POSITIVE PRACTICE.*** The underlying premise in this approach is that if a child is misbehaving or failing to follow an expectation, then perhaps the child doesn't understand or needs practice in "refining" his or her skill—much like homework helps a student learn how to solve a math problem. Of course wise parents know their children's misbehavior is usually the result of their decision to misbehave rather than not understanding what is expected; this is precisely why a disciplinary intervention is required—to let the child know that the parent is still in control and can insist on their cooperation.

In positive practice, parents request that a child practice a behavior they wish to see improved. This intervention can help the child recognize he or she can accomplish the behavior with very little effort when motivated to accomplish it. For example, if a youngster always forgets to turn off lights when leaving a room, parents might ask the child to practice four or five times to help him or her remember this important lesson in energy conservation.

Parents must remember, though, that positive practice should truly be "positive" in nature. If a child is forced to practice excessively and the focus becomes punitive, then the intervention becomes punishment rather than discipline and loses its educational component. Positive practice is most effective when it truly ***inconveniences the child***; it should occur on the child's time, for example, during his or her favorite television program or after beginning to play a video game. I recommend allowing the program to start and after about 5 or 10 minutes into the program, then announcing "it's practice time!" Explain to the child which skill you've observed that needs some practice and indicate that upon completion of the practice session, he or she can resume their activity. Misbehavior usually takes place at a time that is inconvenient for the parent—you know, right before bedtime, or 5 minutes prior to the bus coming for school pick-up, or on the morning a parent has an important meeting at work, etc. Positive practice, on the other hand, takes place when inconvenient for the child and fairly convenient for the parent; this helps the parent keep it "light and cheerfully positive." After all, it is not the parent's misbehavior—but the child's!

Positive practice has been effective in altering problematic bedtime behaviors, eliminate dawdling on school mornings which could make the student late for school, better control sibling rivalry problems which are typical of siblings, correct non-compliance with household rules, improving room cleanliness, and a host of other typical parent-child challenges during the parenting years.

## **The Productive Use of Anxiety**

Anxiety can be a very uncomfortable state, and most people will work toward eliminating it. When anxious, people start exploring options that might lower such feelings, and it is this same anxiety that causes many of us to change our behavior. First of all, let us be reassured that using anxiety productively and therapeutically will not escalate into "panic attacks" or "generalized anxiety" that would be considered an emotional problem. We are simply suggesting that some anxiety can be utilized by parents to make their children a little uncomfortable or ill at ease about misbehavior.

Children need a predictable environment with consistent expectations that should not change from day to day or from parent to parent; child development experts tell us this adds to a child's security, sense of well being, and feelings of adequacy. It is ***unpredict-ability*** that produces therapeutic anxiety for children. Parents often become too predictable in their discipline; then children experience little discomfort even over their misbehavior. Instead of fearing a consequence, the child already knows the consequence for the misbehavior and therefore begins calculating and making decisions. For example, if Johnny knows that he simply gets a lecture on kindness every time he hits his sister, there will be times he will weigh the advantages of hitting her and then gearing up for the lecture. Now on the other hand, if he isn't sure what the consequence for that misbehavior will be, he will stop and think about it and perhaps decide not to take the chance since the consequence is not so predictable.

Another means of being unpredictable as parents involve ***switching roles in administering discipline*** rather than fall into patterns such as one parent being the "good guy" and the other the "bad guy." It's seems more fair to have both parents share the good guy—bad guy continuum. While both parents should attempt to show a united front with the child, one parent can be the primary spokesperson for administering the discipline with the other parent taking a supportive role and encouraging the child to cooperatively fulfill the consequence so he or she can resume normal activities. The next occasion when discipline is needed, perhaps the roles can be reversed by mom and dad. As parents are less predictable in parental roles regarding discipline, the potential for adding therapeutic anxiety is possible and thus the disciplinary intervention more effective.

Most parents quickly react and announce the discipline they have chosen for their son or daughter, and by so doing, they do not allow time for the child to contemplate or think about his or her misbehavior. If parents are too predictable, the child learns quickly how to manipulate the system and quite often decides to misbehave and accept the consequence he knows will follow. A child who knows the system this well has little anxiety over misbehavior. Once having such power or control, the child learns manipulative behaviors which he or she can then use to control his parents and others as well. While expectations for behavior should be consistent, the manner in which parents choose to respond in ***disciplinary measures***

***must be unpredictable*** and perhaps even ***inconsistent to be more powerful and effective***.

## *Postponement of Discipline Is Effective Tool*

***Delaying the consequence*** is another important concept for parents to practice in their disciplinary decisions. While a crisis or misbehavior may have to be stopped, the subsequent discipline does not have to be announced until a parent has had time to calm down, think through the most appropriate, creative discipline they can think of, and when possible even discuss it with the other parent to maximize their teamwork abilities. In over 25 years of practice, I've never met a parent yet, that can produce the best disciplinary intervention at the time of the crisis. Most of us need some time to get our emotions under control and think logically about the situation. When we try to handle the problem immediately, we are impulsive; ***we react rather than respond*** to the misbehavior. Good discipline is the result of ***responding to the problem, rather than reacting***! Parents also tend to show their anger or frustration in a reacting mode; the child then focuses his or her thinking on how "out of control" the parent is rather than thinking about the inappropriate decision made. Parents need to learn to intervene by stopping the crisis, but to postpone giving the discipline until a later time after both parent and child has had a time to calm down and thus be more objective in considering the problem or conflict.

## *Therapeutic Anxiety*

This "waiting" period of time, which is recommended above, ***produces some anxiety for the child*** as he or she knows some discipline will be forthcoming, but not sure what it will be. I encourage parents to even tell the child that while he or she is awaiting the disciplinary decision, they should think of a possible discipline since the parent may actually choose to ask the child for suggestions. Many times, the child will come up with a more severe discipline than the one proposed by the parent and so the parent appears more fair, flexible, and less harsh. The goal of discipline is to get the child thinking about the inappropriate decision made, why it was wrong, and alternatives for handling the situation in the future. This "waiting" time allows this thinking to take place and therefore makes the discipline far more effective.

A good example of the effectiveness of "therapeutic anxiety" for us adults would involve being signaled to pull off the road by the red flashing light on the state trooper's car that is following us when we know we have exceeded the speed limit on a given highway. From the moment that I notice the light until the whole ordeal is over, I get quite anxious. The reason for my anxiety is not so much that I could have to pay $100 in a traffic ticket, but it's the uncertain outcome that makes me uncomfortable. I realize the officer represents ultimate power on the highway—he could give me a warning, give me a ticket, or even worse, confuse me for someone else and call in back-up and frisk me and search my car for drugs, etc. Not being able to predict the outcome is what produces anxiety for me; and, I dare say is the reason I choose to drive within the speed limit since I will do just about anything to avoid that uncomfortable feeling of anxiety. Here, anxiety helps me make better decisions and helps me control my behavior. This same therapeutic anxiety can help children make better decisions and is therefore an effective tool to be utilized by parents during the parenting years.

## The Stop...Think...Do...Program

With the rather epidemic levels of what is known as Attention Deficit Hyperactivity Disorder (ADHD) and Attention Deficit Disorder (ADD) among our children in this culture, a large number of parents struggle with finding behavioral interventions that will help them teach their children to be less impulsive and think through problem solving rather than impulsively react. Whether a child has been identified and diagnosed with ADD or ADHD or perhaps just one prone to the normal impulsivity that characterizes high energy youngsters during the growing up years, the Stop...Think...Do... Program (2) is an excellent disciplinary tool for such situations. It also helps to teach children problem solving skills by learning how to "respond" to problems rather than to "react" to them. Based on the assumption that good decisions are made in 3 simple steps, the child is taught to: *(1) STOP, (2) THINK, and (3) DO or proceed.*

As a visual aid, the Stop…Think…Do…Program can utilize the traffic light with red signaling STOP, yellow signaling THINK, and then of course, green signaling GO or Proceed. Some parents have even helped teach this program through hand motions with the child placing his or her hand up like a police officer directing traffic for "STOP," then pointing to his or her head for "THINK," and finally thrusting the hand forward for signaling "DO" or "PROCEED." In working with children experiencing ADHD or ADD in therapy, we often make stickers and posters with this wording so that the child can be exposed to such reminders throughout the day. At school, typically the teacher will permit the ADHD child to place a sticker on his or her notebook or desk to serve as a visual reminder to solve problems rather than react to them.

When confronting a child who has impulsively reacted to a problem, parents or teachers can first ask the child, "Did you stop and think about that problem before you made your decision?" If parents and other significant persons in the child's life (teachers, baby sitters, grandparents, etc.) consistently use this same approach to confront the misbehavior, the child begins to respond to this form of thinking and begins incorporating this practice into his or her own decision making. The Stop…Think…Do…Program is an excellent format for the discussion that should be a part of all discipline; it provides a system for the parent to discuss the misbehavior and teach the value they wish to convey during this very important component of discipline.

## Reversal of Responsibility

*Reversal of responsibility places accountability for behavior on the child* rather than allowing parents to assume responsibility. Parents sometimes get so upset with the child that they react negatively, in frustration and anger. The child then focuses on the adult's anger rather than why the behavior was wrong. Parents should be *simple and direct when confronting a problem*; as much as possible, they should *try to remain calm, objective, and non-emotional!* This approach will convey to the child that the problem is his or her responsibility rather than the parent's. Parents could address such a situation with one of the following questions:

## *Sample Questions To Ask In Confronting Child*

"Who is responsible for your behavior?"
"Who did it?"
"How could you have handled the problem differently?"
"Did you STOP and THINK before you made your decision?"
"Will you handle it that way the next time this problem
    happens?"

Children would rather focus on the reason for misbehavior as opposed to accepting responsibility they need to assume for having performed it. Parents need to be alert to excuses or irrelevant issues that change the focus or serve to avoid responsibility. If parents react out of frustration, then children quickly focus on how out of control the parent is rather than the misbehavior that is the real problem. Impulsively reacting to the child's misbehavior can appear as if the parent is feeling responsible for the child's misbehavior. As already discussed in a previous section, by delaying the disciplinary action, parents are given time to "cool off" and gain their objectivity; they also have time to be more creative in thinking about the appropriate disciplinary action. Implementation of the *discipline can then be done in a rather non-emotional and objective manner*; after all, it is the child's behavior that produced the need for this consequence and if he or she corrects it, further disciplinary actions will not be necessary.

## **Natural and Logical Consequences**

The essence of *natural consequences is to let children learn from experience or nature*. For example, a child learns by being stung that bees are dangerous; refusing to eat lunch brings about mid-afternoon hunger pains. Natural consequences, although they are quite effective learning tools, have limitations! Very few parents would allow a child to learn from experience that jumping into a deep swimming pool without any swimming lessons would not be healthy. Nor would parents allow children to learn about electricity by permitting them to play with or around an electrical outlet. Most parents would try to protect their child from a playmate who would demonstrate the true meaning of "an eye for an eye" in response to aggression.

*Logical consequences are similar to natural consequences in that consequences are linked to behavior, most likely through a logical, verbal explanation by the parent.* For example, it is quite logical that a child who misuses a pool table (an expensive piece of recreational equipment for the family rec-room) not be permitted to use it until he or she can demonstrate the responsibility and maturity necessary to use the equipment appropriately.

A child who plays hooky from school should be asked to make up the schoolwork on Saturday morning or after school, not as a punitive measure but as a logical one. Because important learning time was misused, the time must be made up. In logical consequences, the parent simply explains that special activities or watching television can take place after homework but not before; "first things must be first," and homework is more important than free time. Logical consequences are also usually understood in advance by the child (for example, "As soon as your homework is done, you can watch television, go out to play, etc.").

## **Mediation Training**

Similar to the Stop…Think…Do…Program for helping reduce impulsive decision making, another important technique that helps children learn through discipline is known as mediation training, which is a way of teaching children self-control (3). An underlying assumption of mediation training is that a child thinks in at least three ways: (1) with words, (2) with mental images, and (3) with motor movements. A child can learn mediation training through these pathways. However, for most children, the verbal thinking approach seems most economical. *Through mediation training*, children are taught self-control by *helping them think through problems by asking the following four questions:*

*1. What did you do wrong?* (problem identification)

*2. What happens when you (name of misbehavior) that you don't like?* (consequence)

*3. What should you have been doing?* (alternatives)

*4. What happens that you like when you (name of appropriate behavior)?* (future planning)

This process of the 4 questions should only take about 5 minutes; anything longer than 5 minutes becomes a "lecture" and the effectiveness of the process diminishes immensely when children feel their parents are merely lecturing or preaching at them. Again, it is important for the parent to maintain an objective, non-emotional approach when utilizing this intervention to help a child learn better ways to solve problems and learn from the experiences of misbehavior.

Although quite a young and inexperienced parent and not truly understanding this concept, I would frequently require a small discussion with my pre-school aged son (Scott) following misbehavior. In his case, and probably true for many children, he rather hated these discussions. I can remember his words to this day, "Daddy do we have to talk about it...?" It appeared that he would rather have accepted some form of a punishment, get it over with so he could resume his playtime, rather than discuss his decision even briefly. As a young parent, I soon realized this was a good intervention and further developed this approach to be used with him clear through his high school years.

## Power Struggles

Avoiding power struggles is such an important principle in parenting, yet a very difficult one to achieve for most parents. *Parents should try to teach children rather than try forcing them to comply*. By inviting a child to participate or help them, parents increase the potential for cooperation on the child's part. Rather than ordering a child by stating, "You do that!" a wise parent suggests "Let's do this...I'll help you!" Children seem to cooperate better and respond to "I'll help you clean up your room..." as opposed to "Clean up your room this instant, or else...!"

Many times when a parent says "or else," the child is tempted to find out more about "or else," and it becomes a challenge for further study and experimentation. Parents should have high expectations for their children, believe in them, and expect them to be great. *Expecting "greatness" rather than "obedience" can make a world of difference in the response one gets from a child.* In over 25 years of practice and having seen literally thousands of children by this point in my career, I've never met a child that didn't want to be great. However, a fairly high percentage of children have more important things on their mind than obedience. As explained in an earlier chapter, the relationship a parent has with the child is the strongest tool the parent has in gaining compliance of the child. A good relationship with a child and support of his or her strengths can go a long way toward avoiding power struggles. *Power struggles are worthless; they lead to nothing but further frustration, conflict, oppositional or rebellious behavior, resentment, and anger.* Absolutely no one wins in a power struggle—neither the parent nor the child! Parents must also remember to avoid making threats that cannot be enforced.

## Additional Miscellaneous Techniques

### *Anticipating Problems*

There are several additional disciplinary techniques worth mentioning. The first of these techniques is *anticipating problems. Parents should try to foresee a problem before it occurs and plan accordingly in an effort to better manage the problem* or prevent it from occurring all together. For example, a family vacation that requires six hours of travel time will most likely result in bored and fidgeting children. A wise parent plans several in-car games, stopping for a snack, or play time at a park somewhere during the trip.

## Hurdle Help

*Hurdle help* increases motivation; it amounts to **giving a child a little "lift" to help him or her feel more like doing something.** Parents show interest in their son's or daughter's science projects, perhaps by helping collect a few of the insects they need. This not only demonstrates their interest in the project but gives extra help, which encourages them to get started and to complete the task.

## The Value of Humor

**Humor works well to defuse a difficult or stressful situation.** It is most important to laugh with children—not at them! Make sure your children know you are **laughing with them and at whatever the situation is rather than at them,** for the latter is an attack on their self-esteem.

## Games

**Putting things in a game context often works well,** especially with necessary responsibilities that aren't very motivating. For example, "Let's see how fast we can rake up the leaves so we can be finished by the time Mom comes home—then we can all go out for ice cream," or "You take that half while I take this one, and let's see who can finish first for the prize of a milkshake—loser buys the milkshake."

## A Booster Shot Of Affection

When a child feels down, perhaps after receiving a poor grade on a test or some other disappointment, he or she needs a **boost of affection.** A **warm comment, an arm around the shoulder,** *a good word conveying your pride* in him or her are all good examples of affection that tends to boost the child's spirit.

## *Signaling*

*Signaling* also works well within a family context. The family can agree on *signals that mean certain things and are well understood* by all family members (for example, a finger to the lip could signal things are getting too loud, a wink of an eye could mean you are proud, etc.). Signaling can be a powerful tool for parents or teachers. I can still remember a signal that my kindergarten teacher used to quiet a noisy room — flipping the light switch off, then back on.

## *Punch & Burp Approach To Discipline*

To confront misbehavior and minimize the potential negative effect of focusing on misbehavior rather than appropriate behavior, parents can adopt a practice known as the *punch and burp approach* to discipline. A *"punch"* is not literally hitting the child, but rather *a figurative expression for a confrontation of misbehavior*; the *"burp"* is a *figurative expression for a compliment of a positive behavior or attribute*. In practice, parents should always attempt to use "burping" when feeling it necessary to "punch" the child for misbehavior; thus, the parental intervention can be more balanced and not all negative or punitive in nature. The following dialogue conveys this approach:

## Punch & Burp Dialogue

"Lee, I'm really so proud to see you play on your team. You really make me proud of your skills; but even more than that, I love to see the way you handle yourself. You really look and act so mature (the burp). I sure wish you could do as well in your social skills — you know, the way you treat your sister. You could really help her in many ways, but you often put her down. How can you be so good, mature, and act so grown-up in sports, yet act so childish toward your sister (the punch)?"

Although it doesn't come naturally with most parents since people in our society don't approach problem solving in this manner, potentially parents can develop the skill so well that they automatically approach any kind of disciplinary challenge with this process. They have successfully broken a typical trap of only confronting the inappropriate behaviors or focusing on the "negative" things. The *"punch and burp" technique helps the parent address the behavior that needs to be confronted while also reinforcing the positives, thus creating a more balanced approach and warmer home environment.*

## Positive Approaches To Discipline

The following 36 positive approaches to discipline are adapted from Saf Lerman's Parent Awareness Training (4).

1. *State your expectations:* Let children know what you expect. Too often adults assume that a child knows what they want, and the child doesn't. Be direct and clear in letting children know what you expect of them.
2. *Be encouraging:* Use encouraging phrases that show you are confident that children can live up to your expectations. Examples of positive ways to phrase your expectations follow:
   a. "It would be helpful if..."
   b. "I have confidence that..."
   c. "I expect you to..."
   d. "I know you can..."
3. *Appreciate improvements:* Let children know that you notice and appreciate their efforts when they correct misbehavior and show they are able to cooperate.
4. Spend a great deal of time *praising, acknowledging, and appreciating* a child's desirable behavior. This encourages and reinforces it.

5. Adults can help to change unacceptable behavior by *making environmental changes*:
   a. If the children are bored, help them to set up construc-tive activities
   b. If the environment has become too stimulating and active, redirect the children to a quiet activity
   c. If the children are hungry, feed them; if they're tired, adjust sleep schedules

6. *Prepare children for changes and transitions:* They will cooperate better if they've had time to adjust. For example, "In ten minutes we'll be leaving for the park, so get your shoes on" or "This weekend we are going on a visit; let's think about what you'll need to take with you on our trip."

7. *Consider the effect of any emotional stresses* on the children's behavior, and give them plenty of opportunity to work through their feelings in appropriate ways.

8. *Keep in mind the age and stage capabilities* of chil-dren and what they are emotionally ready to handle. Try not to ask too much or too little of a child. Adults often believe young children can handle more than they really can. When there is a recurring conflict over the same situation, it could indicate that a child is not capable of what you are asking. Being familiar with developmental stages can keep your expectations realistic.

9. *Distract:* Don't mention the child's misbehavior, but direct his or her attention elsewhere.

10. *Avoid asking a young child questions that encourage a "no" answer* and a possible attack of rebelliousness. Instead of asking, "Do you want to put your shoes on?" be firm and say, "It's time to get your shoes on now."

11. *Be clear and emphatic* when you need to be. Say "You must wear your winter jacket this morning. There is no choice about it!"

12. *Stay simple:* Don't make a long speech when a stern glance or brief "Cut it out" is all that is needed.

13. *State the limit impersonally:* "Walls are not for writing on" is better than "You may not write on walls." This puts the focus on the rule, not the child.

14. *Offer alternatives:* Children need to know what they can do, not merely what they cannot do. For example, "The chair is not for jumping on. You can jump on the floor." or "People are not for hitting. Hit this pillow instead."

15. *Bend your rules for special occasions:* For example, if bedtime is usually 8:30 and a special television show is on until later or there are special circumstances, you can extend the bedtime hour, thereby showing flexibility.

16. *Give the reasons* for your rules and limits.

17. According to the child and the solution, *it may be necessary to repeat the limit.*

18. *Give children the chance to express their feelings* about a situation before expecting them to try and resolve it.

19. *Allow a child in fantasy what he or she can't be allowed in reality:* "You wish you were grown up and could go to bed much later, but now it's really your bedtime."

20. *Teach the child to use words* instead of hits, kicks, or bites when angry: "You were angry at Jerry, but he is not for hitting; use words to tell him you are mad at him."

21. When a child needs a more forceful outlet than words for anger and aggression, encourage him or her to hit a pillow and help the child to verbalize angry feelings while doing so. *Work toward physical outlets for anger* that do not involve hitting, like jumping rope, jogging, weight lifting, or some other physical activity.

22. *Give a warning:* Warn children of the effect their behavior is having upon you: "Right now I am still a pleasant person, but in a few minutes, if this keeps up, you'll have an angry person to deal with."

23. *Tell the child you are angry when you are:* Giving your honest disapproval lets children understand the consequences of their behavior, and they will feel more secure when you respond in an honest way about your feelings.

24. *Use statements that express mutual cooperation:* For example, "If you cooperate and let me finish this report, then I will cooperate with your request for me to play your game."

25. When you are in the middle of an argument over insignificant matters, *erase the scene and start again.* Leave the room, come back, and pretend the conflict never happened.

26. *Offer choices:* "You have a choice. You can play ball outside or stay inside and pick something else to do." *Choices should be clear-cut, and the parent must be prepared to follow through.* If the child remains indoors and continues to throw the ball, the parent needs to take the ball away, saying, "You decided to stay inside; go do something else." Choices help children become more responsible for their decisions.

27. *Tell children how their behavior is affecting you,* and then leave them to think of a way to remedy the situation on their own. Instead of saying, "Please turn down the radio so I can hear," a parent could say, "I can't hear on the telephone with the radio so loud" and allow the child to figure out what needs to be done, whether it's closing doors, turning down the volume, or taking the radio to another room.

28. *Whenever feasible, give children some control:* As children get older, they need some flexibility. Parents could offer, "You can do your homework whenever you want to, as long as it's done before you watch television or play video games."

29. *Begin your request with as soon as:* "As soon as you put your toys away, you can watch television" or "As soon as you brush your teeth, I'll read you a story."

30. *Use role reversal:* Role reversals in which the adult and child pretend to be each other can be very effective. You can reverse roles just for the fun of it at times and also in discipline situations. Children feel powerful playing the adult role, and then return to being the child refreshed. A child should not be forced to reverse roles; this technique only works when the child desires to do so—it's not worth

a power struggle. A child can play the adult for a short time without being on the spot. This gives the child a few extra moments to think the issue through. By playing the adult role, a child gets to set his or her own limit and will often pay more attention to it when it is self-formulated. Switching roles, lightens the tone, too. Even very young children can appreciate the humor of an adult pretending to be a "child having a tantrum."

31. *Be humorous:* Humor can be a great aid in solving conflicts, whenever the parent feels up to it. Children of all ages appreciate humor at their level.

32. *Use a game-like approach* to enliven routine tasks. Get ideas from television game shows like *Beat the Clock* or use games of chance; for example, everyone who is up, dressed, and completes his or her chores by a certain time gets to draw a number for a prize.

33. *Put some requests in writing:* When children begin to read, occasionally having a request in writing can make it easier to accept. For example, "Dear Jason, You said your clothes would be left in the hamper, not on the floor. How about it? With love, Dad." The child can be encouraged to write back.

34. *Make a deal!* "You can stay up until nine o'clock if you play quietly in your room while we have dinner with our company. Otherwise, you'll need to go to bed at your regular time. Is it a deal?"

35. *From time to time, bribe:* Occasionally, bribing is a reasonable way of making the situation easier for parents. For example, "If you are pleasant and cooperative while I go to the supermarket, I'll buy you an ice cream cone on the way home" or " If you go to bed on time tonight so I can enjoy my company, you'll find a surprise in your shoe tomorrow morning."

36. *Approach issues as problems to solve:* Adults can encourage children to think of ways to solve a problem and often the children will come up with excellent, orig-inal solutions. If not, the adults can offer positive solu-

tions themselves and include the children in the process of deciding from among them. It's good to agree on a solution acceptable to all. Adults can rely on this approach more and more as children grow older. It's much easier for children to comply with a decision if they helped to make it and their needs were genuinely respected in the process.

# Chapter 9

# Sticking To Essentials

꙾

*Fathers [and mothers], do not exasperate your children; instead,*
*bring them up in the training and instruction of the Lord.*
*Ephesians 6:4*

A rather popular expression that is really very good advice to parents is *"DON'T SWEAT THE SMALL STUFF!"* Far too often, parents tend to lose objectivity and begin over emphasizing or over-reacting to non essential things. Making mountains out of pimples will nearly destroy the relationship a parent has established with a son or daughter; and, thus should be avoided at all costs.

All the essential issues of parenting have never been covered in any single volume, and this book is not an attempt to achieve that nearly impossible goal. However, this chapter is a collection of essentials for Christian parenting that will provide additional insight regarding parenting tasks.

## Delight In Your Children

"Delighting" simply means accepting one's children as they are, spontaneously expressing affection for who they are and not what they have accomplished. Children need plenty of free hugs and attention from their parents. Thomas Mullins, a Quaker minister who authored *When 2 or 3 Are Gathered Together Someone Spills The Milk*, says that parents can learn to love their children despite spilled milk. Our children can at times make us so proud that loving them is easy. It is those times when their angelic qualities disappear that delighting in them becomes more of a challenge. Those uninhibited youngsters who tell all the family secrets that were never intended to go beyond the door of the home (let alone to the backyard, the neighborhood, the school, the church, or the in-laws) make delighting quite difficult. Regardless of trying situations, delighting must be a part of every parent-child relationship.

As parents, we must not forget to enjoy our children even in those trying moments. If we only pause for a moment, laugh with our kids, and have some fun with them, we would discover how wonderfully made they really are. By taking notice of our children, we prepare ourselves to handle even the largest challenge that might try our patience. Delighting helps parents look at problems as opportunities.

Because we live in such a fast-paced society, it is easy to miss important moments that can help us and our children grow. Lest we are too busy, let us make planned and concentrated efforts to take notice of our children. Although psychological research confirms that parental warmth is associated positively with the child developing high self-esteem, many parents spend only a few minutes per day in child focused functions or activities. Self-worth is one of the most important elements of our children's emotional health, and delighting in them is a good way to build their self-esteem and self-confidence.

## Respect Your Children

People should be respected, and children are people too! Parents and other adults should treat children with much care, not misleading or discouraging them in any way. Adults often do things to children that they would never think of doing to another adult. Adults often ignore, belittle, or criticize children needlessly and usually without regard for their feelings. Those same adults would not attempt to administer such treatment to one of their peers, but children are expected to grin and bear it.

I have often seen parents make feeble attempts at disciplining their children in public by ridiculing them in front of peers or other people. Such poor parenting is usually ineffective as discipline; furthermore it is doubly destructive to that child's self-worth. In such situations, a child often tries to save face with peers or defend his or her ego by openly challenging or resisting the parent, which results in a power struggle where neither the parent nor child wins.

Parents should always discipline in private if possible. I don't buy the excuse some parents use that if children misbehave in public they deserve to be disciplined in public. In such situations, one needs to examine the motivation behind the discipline. Is the goal for the child to internalize a value to apply in future situations or is it for all to see that the parent is a good parent who disciplines his or her children? Still worse, is the discipline given in anger by a parent who feels better after confronting the child? Public discipline of a child does not lead to admiration of the parent. I've often wanted to give those parents my business card and suggest a private therapy session to discuss appropriate disciplinary interventions.

Several years ago, I attended an evangelistic crusade in Columbus, Ohio. While waiting for the service to start one evening, I amused myself by observing the people sitting around me. I especially enjoyed watching a little toddler make her way from a row of seats down to the front of the auditorium. I was even further amused that her parents, who were socializing with friends, had not noticed her departure from their seats. After discovering that the child was missing and being chagrined at her whereabouts, the embarrassed father made his way down to the front of the auditorium, picked the little girl up and raised her above his head to swat her on the rump three or four times. My amusement quickly changed to anger. I'm sure the real goal behind such a display was to make Dad feel less embarrassed rather than to have the toddler internalize the value of staying in her seat while attending crusades.

## Admit Errors & Ask Forgiveness When Wrong

Some parents act as though they never err; others are too proud or ashamed to admit they make errors. Still other parents admit error to peers but never to their children. Admitting to others when one is wrong is not a sign of weakness but one of strength. None of us are perfect, but only some of us are honest and mature enough to admit our faults. Recognizing errors and admitting responsibility takes courage; however, it is the first step toward remediation of the mistake.

When parents admit mistakes to their children, they are modeling humanity and humility—both good qualities to teach children. By asking forgiveness, parents model not only that they are human and sometimes make errors, but that they are honest in accepting responsibility for changing wrongs. In many respects, a parent's error can be a golden opportunity to model and teach significant values in positive interpersonal relationships. There is nothing more healing for a family than the act of asking a loved one's forgiveness. Asking a child to forgive us can demonstrate a deep respect for the child and absolutely works toward enhancing the parent-child relationship.

## Give Children Opportunities To Provide Input & Help Make Decisions

Parents should encourage their children to take an active part in the family by allowing them to provide input regarding family decisions. Psychological research reports that children with high self-esteem often come from homes that are democratic, with every member of the family participating in some decision making. Of course, parents must retain their God-given responsibility to oversee the family, asking for input on appropriate issues and making judicious use of suggestions.

If parents practice this principle and look for opportunities where children can have a part in decision making, the children will learn about decision making, cooperation, and the democratic process a well as feel involved and an important part of the family. Most adults would refuse to participate on a committee or work crew that was run the way some parents run their families. Industries promote participatory management—getting input from all who are involved and letting them participate in decision making. Such a process usually yields much better output; most people find it easier to support something they have helped to create. Families that are more participatory will probably experience fewer heartaches resulting from childhood rebellion.

Parents should look for opportunities to elicit involvement of the children, for example, vacations and weekend events. Children should be kept abreast of family finances and situations that limit the range of such activities, such as a pay cut, the loss of a job, illness or increased medical costs, or mom's pregnancy, etc.

## Build Family Traditions

Edith Schaeffer talks about building a "museum of memories" which are the traditions that are remembered by children long after they have left home. These traditions from their family of origin, will probably be practiced in their own homes and passed down to their children as well. Traditions include the manner in which a family celebrates birthdays, whether they open gifts on Christmas Eve or Christmas Day, and recognition or celebration of special events in the family's life. The value we place on little league baseball games, hiking through the park, saying or singing grace at the dinner table, or riding bikes on Sunday afternoon will determine whether such activities become family traditions. Primary among family traditions should be establishing the importance of family devotional times.

I have found that it is not necessarily the expensive activities that are remembered by children. Even though trips to a rather expensive amusement park will be cherished by all members of the family, creative, inexpensive activities can have equal value if done in a manner that makes them memorable. The important element isn't the money spent but the fellowship that family members share which makes an event significant to each member. Riding bikes, flying kites, walking through the park, or just taking a drive to the Dairy Queen after yard work on a hot Saturday afternoon can achieve this goal without taxing the family budget. Family activities become traditions precisely because they have meaning and value to family members.

Other family traditions we practice combine necessary household duties with play and social interaction. For example, when my son was still at home, he and I would always mow the grass together. As a young child, his involvement was quite limited and actually lengthened rather than shortened the time required for the task. Many times, he would ride in the wheel barrow on the way back from dumping grass trimmings or be pulled in his wagon while mowing. As he matured, however, he was able to take on more responsibility and later assumed the bulk of this task with some assistance from me. I never will forget the day he asked me to mow the back yard while he attended to the front yard as he expressed as sensitively as possible, "Dad, your rows aren't quite as straight as mine...the neighbors know I mow the lawn and I want them to see straight lines." You see, he had developed landscaping skills that now exceeded the teacher and I was pleased to assume a secondary role as he assumed the major responsibility for this task. I was also very pleased that he had adopted high quality standards for his performance. My work as a parent had been successful; he was now skilled at my level and beyond.

Prioritizing such practices not only legitimizes the family and the importance of each member but marks the importance of establishing family memories. Traditions help us remember significant events and values, and gives meaning to parents' teaching. Our memories of the family help us prioritize the values of the family as well as keep those priorities straight as we complete necessary responsibilities. In a day when the significance of family is diminishing rapidly, it is crucial that Christian parents preserve its significance.

## Spend Time With Your Children

Some parents try to fulfill their role in the most efficient way they can—doing as little as possible or contracting the function out to others. This is not to criticize the use of day-care centers, preschools, or babysitters, for they are necessary when both parents work. But parents must take sufficient time to perform the tasks related to the role of parenting. Most parents have heard that "quality time" is more important than the "quantity" of time spent with their children. However, the tasks of parenting do take time, and responsibilities must be prioritized in a way that allows sufficient time for this ultimately important aspect of the parenting role.

*Quality time is giving a youngster undivided attention.* The child receiving quality time feels they are the most important focus and distractions won't interfere with the parent's attention to him or her. It conveys to the child that he or she is a most important person and that the parent cares and is concerned about the child's interests. In many cases, if a child feels that he or she has a parent's undivided attention for a few minutes that child will be satisfied and allow the parent to return to reading the paper or watching the evening news.

Unfortunately, it is not unusual for parents to minister to their child's needs while doing something else as well. Usually the child recognizes that the news has higher priority than a game or tea party. Even though a parent may have spent a reasonable quantity of time with a child, the value is limited if the child feels he or she had to compete with some other activity. Some parents tell me that they spend enormous amounts of time with their children and in desperation say, "It seems like the more time I spend with her, the more she demands of me—she just never gets enough attention." These parents may be giving quantity time rather than quality time. Try joining your children for Saturday morning cartoons for an hour or so; you might be surprised at how enjoyable such an activity can be. You will probably be given the remaining morning hours to accomplish other necessary tasks without much interference from the children since their needs have been met.

## Listen, Listen, Listen, and Listen Again!

There is probably no more important element in communication than listening, for true communication involves more listening than talking. Parents need to remember that communication includes both verbal and nonverbal behaviors. It is very frustrating and aggravating for parents to talk to a child who is obviously not paying attention. However, this same phenomenon can involve the parent who is only partially listening to the child. While saying they are listening, their nonverbal behaviors strongly suggest they are distracted or otherwise focused on other things. If it is the parent who is merely going through the motions of listening, the child may become frustrated with and angry at the parent. About 70-80% of our communication is nonverbal and only about 20-30% is verbal. So rather than just telling a child we are interested in listening to them, we must act like it. Parents must attend to their nonverbal behaviors!

Children often get the impression that what they have to say is unimportant because adults seem to ignore them or disregard their conversations or questions. Perhaps they have even heard from their parents the old saying, "Children are to be seen and not heard." I'm not implying that children should be made a part of every adult conversation for such would be inappropriate. However, if children feel a part of discussions where appropriate, they may exhibit fewer attention-getting behaviors that interfere with adult conversations.

Parents might get to know their children better if they listen to them. If parents stop long enough to listen to what their children are saying to them and each other, they truly know them; and by knowing their children, parents better understand them. By better understanding them, they are more capable of establishing a better relationship with them!

## Avoid Power Struggles and Be Fair

Parents should save their threats. Generally, parents regret having made them and usually make them at a time when they are angry. Many threats are impossible to carry out. Quite often, parents will say they're going to do things that they really can't do, should not do, or do not even wish to do. More importantly, threats move us from a position of relationships and a powerful influence to one of no choice and generally right smack dab into a power struggle, where the youngster has far more of the share of power. After all, the child can always act "childish," but the adult is not permitted to act immature or irresponsible.

Power struggles quite often encourage the child to obey maliciously or "smart off," but still be doing what was asked of him. Dobson, in a film series entitled *Turn Your Heart Toward Home*, tells a story about a family on a vacation trip. The two children start the trip with great expectations; however, as the trip progresses, they become bored and start acting out and disregard warnings from their father. Finally, in desperation, the father stops the car, takes both children out of the car and spanks them, telling them he doesn't want hear a word out of them for the next two hours. After two hours, the little boy gracefully asks his father, "Is it okay to talk now?" Once granted permission by his father, the young lad says, "When you spanked me back there two hours ago, I lost my shoe as you put me back into the car. You told me I couldn't say anything, so I didn't." Having a passive aggressive flavor, this is a good example of malicious obedience.

Parents need to be fair! If parents didn't see what happened, they should not make assumptions just because it has happened this way several times before. If this is the exception to the pattern, blaming the child in error may be devastating to the parent-child relationship and something the child will never forget. Although we as parents might be able to forget about it, the child who was blamed for something he didn't do is traumatized and quite likely to remember the trauma forever.

Parents also need to focus on the positive rather than the negative. Parents violate this rule by ignoring their youngsters until they misbehave, thus focusing all their attention on incorrect or negative behavior. Far too often, parents utilize such negative statements of control such as "take your feet off that chair" when they could respond in a more positive manner without decreasing any of the assertiveness the response carries. For example, an alternative to such a statement could be, "please put your feet on the floor, where they belong." Other examples include "please place your coat where it belongs" rather than "get your coat off the floor—you don't live in a barn."

## Model Christ

Christ taught the majority of his lessons by example. The importance of modeling has already been emphasized in previous chapters. As parents, we should model the life we hope and pray that our children will learn to live. Parents modeling values, morals, and beliefs will go much further in helping their children identify and internalize these more than any hard-sell lectures or other forms of coercion. If parents model Christ in their everyday living, they will be impressed with the impact it has upon their children's behavior—and, I might add, their own behavior as well!

# Chapter 10

# Remaining Patient During Adolescence

꾳

*But the fruit of the Spirit is love, joy, peace, patience, kindness,
goodness, faithfulness, gentleness, and self control.
Against such things there is no law.
Galations 5:22-23*

No publication on parenting would be complete without spending some time on the period of adolescence, for it is thought to be the most difficult period of all parenting. Some parents are victorious as "good parents" until their children become teenagers, and then it seems as if something radically changes, for they lose their confidence and creativity. After losing confidence in themselves, they seem to accept this developmental period as totally unmanageable. Some parents in desperation disown their teenage children, while others continue to claim them as part of the family but describe them to others as an entity totally beyond reason or understanding.

Regardless of how parents feel about this period of development, it can be challenging to even the best of us. It is a time that taxes our many resources as we attempt to help our children mature in a stormy period of development. Some parents make the mistake of becoming far more concerned than they need to, for they fret and plan for the worst; in short, they set themselves up by requiring compliance to expectations that are totally unreasonable. The manner in which the child responds to parental authority prior to teenage years is much, much different than the manner that can be expected by parents during these stormy, autonomy-seeking years during adolescence.

Some parents expect negative behavior and resistance, and to some extent the teenager begins living up to their parent's expectations. All stages of child development have both their challenges and rewards. Adolescence is no different than other stages in the life cycle, only publicized more. Adolescence is a transition from childhood to early adulthood; it is a period of time that the child will need support in learning to adapt to changes in his or her life, and even throughout the rest of life. Adapting to change isn't merely an adolescent phenomenon.

## A Transitional Stage Of The Life Cycle

Adolescence is by definition a transitional stage, a time when one is no longer a child, yet still not an adult. Teenagers feel and certainly experience that they are "in between" or in a transition. Any life transition can be difficult, stressful, and produce anxiety; all change—even good changes will produce anxiety for most people. Perhaps the adolescent transition is one of the more challenging ones in that the adolescent has very little experience in making transitions. Up to this point in his or her life, transitions have been facilitated by parental figures. The changes and transitions that occurred, happened without much input from the child; now during teenage years, the child wishes and needs to be a part of the transition. Since adolescence for most children starts at about twelve or thirteen years of age, a child must begin accomplishing this transition into adulthood without prior experience. Until adolescence, such transitions are merely accepted by the child and facilitated by the parent; now, things are different. Allowing the child, who has remained fairly compliant and silent in previous transitions, input is perhaps as difficult for the parent as it is for the inexperienced teenager who is demanding input.

Rather than being helpful to teens, adults seem to increase stress by frequently telling them to "grow up," "be more mature," or "stop acting like a child." However, the moment a young man or woman tries to do this, the adults send inconsistent messages, which only add to the young person's confusion and frustration. Frequent messages sent by adults to teenagers include, "You're really not old enough to do this"… "When you get older you can take on this responsibility"… "Now that you're a teenager, you think you know everything about life." These inconsistent messages cause the young person to feel misunderstood; they then begin turning to peers who may be experiencing similar transitional issues and therefore seem to understand them. As young people turn to their friends in desperation and begin to exchange views, they receive understanding, which then strengthens the peer relationship and reinforces a declining respect for parents or adults who don't seem to understand.

## Physical Changes

In addition to being in a state of transition with expectations and roles being redefined, the young person experiences physical, cognitive, and emotional changes—all interacting with each other. *Physical changes* become quite obvious as puberty begins. Not only does the body start changing in appearance but the chemical and hormonal balance shifts to one of extreme activity with hormonal drives during adolescence. These hormonal changes can cause the adolescent to react more emotionally than in prior stages with reactive, angry outbursts, depressive episodes, increased anxiety, and insecurity. A new focus on body image becomes paramount as the young person struggles with acne. The rapid body growth will sometimes cause coordination problems and may cause them to appear "clumsy." Body changes from the enlargement of breasts for girls to the voice changes occurring in males all produce increased anxiety for the young adolescent. All these challenges can pose threats to peer acceptance which is more important than acceptance from family at this stage.

# Cognitive Changes

*Cognitive* changes become apparent as the adolescent begins to think like adults and becomes much more of a challenge to the adults around him or her. The teenager can now go beyond the concrete or simplistic thinking characteristic of early childhood and can now experience abstract thinking like adults. For the first time in a young person's life, he or she becomes concerned about the hypothetical, the future, the remote. Unlike earlier childhood when the parents' word was generally taken as final, the teenager starts to challenge parents' rationale and questions their reasoning. They request explanations and demand the "opportunity to present their case."

The adolescent's behaviors associated with this higher level of thinking (questioning the rationale, demanding explanations, and sometimes expressing disagreement with good documentation and rationale) becomes threatening to the parent. Up to this point, raising children has been fun and exciting; now it becomes challenging! If parents of a young teenager are not careful, they become defensive and react in ways that begin to erode the parent-child relationship they have built through the earlier years of childhood. Preserving and enhancing this relationship is critical, as it will be a support that can enable successfully helping the teenager make this life transition.

# Emotional Changes

*Emotional changes* involve emotional extremes unlike any other stage that preceded this one. Emotionally, adolescents go through many changes. Young people begin thinking of themselves as individuals, apart from parents, and they strive for emancipation or autonomy. As teens strive to pull away from parents, they become preoccupied with acceptance by their social group or peers. Peer influence becomes more important than family.

Although desiring the emotional security and acceptance from parents, most adolescent energies are directed toward the peer group as they worry about physical appearance, attractiveness, and physical development. The teenager's values take on a similarity to those of the peer group as opposed to teachings from family and upbringing. This, of course, further worries parents, who have for the first several years of the child's life tried to teach appropriate values that now seem disregarded.

All these changes are quite challenging to parents who have remained the most significant people in their child's life until now. All of a sudden, a father is discounted as someone who doesn't quite know the way things are in the modern world. Mothers, likewise, have a difficult time understanding their children as they try to be supportive and are pushed away. Power struggles begin, especially when parents refuse to change what has been the normal way of doing things.

## Generation Gap

Sometimes a rift occurs in the parent-child relationship, which has for years been called *the generation gap.* There does not need to be a generational gap between parent and child. However, communication must be kept open and practiced from a very young age if parents wish to have their children enter into adolescence and continue open communication with them. Unfortunately, habits and patterns are hard to change, and usually a poor pattern of communication in early parent-child relationships does not alter itself when the child becomes a teenager. By the time a child enters adolescence, if no one has been truly listening, the child recognizes this and ceases any further efforts. Parents then get overly concerned because their teenagers are secretive, isolated, non-communicative, and share more with friends than family. In essence, the teenager realizes that his parents haven't been listening to him or her, so they just stop trying to share; rather, they share more with their peer group who is listening!

## Parents Must Avoid Pushing Teenager Over The Edge

Despite the challenges adolescence brings for parents, they must cautiously avoid pushing the teenager over the edge! James Dobson in "Focus on the Family" seminars encouraged parents to prepare themselves for helping their children through adolescence by taking every opportunity to tolerate and support them. Parents can take their cue from Scripture: ***Right now it is not pleasant to deal with this problem, yet I know that if my child can gain insight and be more adequately trained through it, this situation will bear fruit in the days ahead (see Hebrews 12:11).***

Parents must accept the fact that it is normal for adolescents to rebel! The rebellion does not have to be aggressive in nature and tends not be so if parents have accepted this phenomenon of adolescence as a natural phase of development. By better preparation on the parent's part, this period of development can be tolerated and lived through by both parents and children as adolescents strive to become independently functioning people who think for themselves. Perhaps parents need to stop trying to force children through development during this period but begin to show acceptance and cooperation.

## COOPERATION Becomes A Key

The simple illustration on the following page depicts the importance of acceptance and cooperation as parents and their adolescent children pursue different goals. Until adolescence, a child generally accepts guidance and direction from parental figures without question. The child never questions the parent; parents find their parenting tasks very easy and even enjoyable as they are "super heroes" to their children. Parents have perfect answers to any question that a child raises; the child proudly accepts his or her parent's answers and guidance for any situation. Then comes adolescence when the youngster starts striving for autonomy and seeking to become his own person.

Beginning to separate him/herself from the family, individualization becomes a major goal in the adolescent's thinking, behavior, and emotions. No longer does the teenager willingly accept the parent's decision; the days for dad or mom to respond with "I'm your parent..." or "I know best..." are over, and they won't return. Instead of responding with unquestionable obedience and never asking for explanations, the adolescent now questions the rationale for the parent's position on issues. Often, the rationale presented by the parent will be challenged; the teenager frequently asks questions that are not easily answered. Instead of demonstrating a simple, concrete level of thinking, the adolescent child is now capable of thinking abstractly—like the parent.

Parents often become defensive in attempting to respond to their son or daughter's new manner of thinking. If not careful, the parent may resort to previous interventions that worked well with the pre-adolescent youngster; if this mistake is made, the result can be disastrous and the gap between parent and child will widen. Allowing their son or daughter to mature into adulthood can be as difficult for the parent as it is for the child. The challenge for parents is to begin talking to the teenager as they do other adults for they are no longer children; talking down to the adolescent can severely hurt the parent-child relationship. On the other hand, the challenge for the teenager is to discard previous "childish" behaviors that worked well in getting their needs met as they acquire the attributes that exhibit maturity and responsibility.

| Parents Insist On Maintaining Traditional Values Taught By Family | ◄◄ ⟵ Parents Pulling One Way<br><br>Teenager Pulling Other Way ⟶ | Teenager's Desire For New Freedoms & Pursuit of Independence |
|---|---|---|

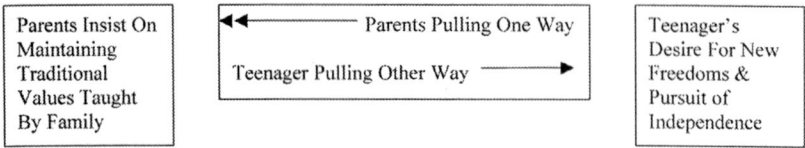

### *Generation Gap Develops*

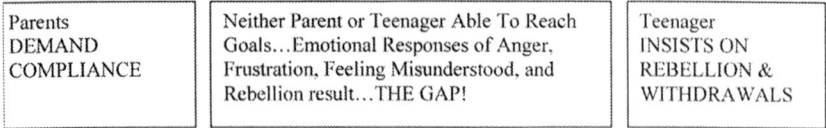

| Parents DEMAND COMPLIANCE | Neither Parent or Teenager Able To Reach Goals...Emotional Responses of Anger, Frustration, Feeling Misunderstood, and Rebellion result...THE GAP! | Teenager INSISTS ON REBELLION & WITHDRAWALS |
|---|---|---|

### *GOAL Is Acceptance & Cooperation*

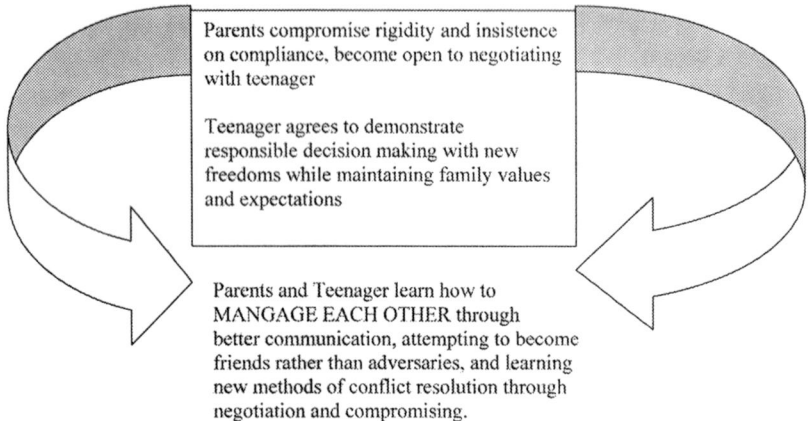

Parents compromise rigidity and insistence on compliance, become open to negotiating with teenager

Teenager agrees to demonstrate responsible decision making with new freedoms while maintaining family values and expectations

Parents and Teenager learn how to MANGAGE EACH OTHER through better communication, attempting to become friends rather than adversaries, and learning new methods of conflict resolution through negotiation and compromising.

# Suggestions For Parenting The Teenager

Starting good parenting practices when a child becomes a teenager will be too late! The ideal parent will start effective parenting practices when the child is brought home from the hospital and even begin thinking about parenting strategies during pregnancy. However, if this has not happened, there are a few suggestions that might help during this time.

## *Parents Should Prepare Themselves For Adolescence By Working Out Their Own Attitude*

First and foremost, parents should prepare themselves for helping their children successfully accomplish adolescence by working out their own attitude regarding this stage of life. Many a parent criticizes their children during adolescence for constantly showing a poor attitude about things, yet they never stop to look at their own, which in many cases is a poor model for their children—often the adult version of what they see and criticize in their son or daughter. Parents must begin thinking differently by trying to expand their level of tolerance during this period of development. Helping a child through adolescence can be an exciting challenge and can truly have a multitude of rewards for the parent who approaches it with a positive attitude.

I can remember one of my more challenging times as a parent to be that of potty training my son. I became quite frustrated in that my psychology training and techniques did not work. The harder I tried, the more frustrated I got! After giving up in frustration and saying that perhaps we had started this process before our son was indeed ready for this teaching, he accomplished on his own what I could not teach him with all my expertise gained from having completed a master's degree in psychology and devoting one entire Saturday to this task. I'm not saying that potty training is more difficult than entering into adolescence but that challenges face us throughout life. Every stage of parenting has its challenges! Such challenges might range from potty training a toddler to school adjustment problems during elementary school, and from autonomy seeking in adolescence to caring for an aged parent in later life. No one period of time in our life cycle need be given credit as the "worst" or "most difficult." Parents need to see adolescence, not as the "worst" time of parenting, but as simply another level with rather unique challenges. Accepting this concept might help to improve our attitude about adolescence.

A parent's attitude is most important! Parents who expect the worst will quite often get the worst. Parents need to be optimistic that they and their children will make it. Parents should probably just relax a little and not become so stressed; when people are stressed, they tend to become reactionary, lose creativity, and become less objective and spontaneous.

## *Accept Emancipation Or Independence Striving As Normal*

Secondly, parents must be willing to accept emancipation or independence striving as normal. Parents certainly want their children to become independent and capable of moving out on their own, holding a responsible job, making responsible decisions, and being respectable law-abiding citizens. Adolescence is a time for sons and daughters to learn these very important skills. Perhaps the many opportunities this period affords a young person will not always turn out to be successful, but parents must not forget they themselves have learned from mistakes. Some of us continue to learn the most important lessons in life from mistakes. Parents should allow some "grace" for legitimate mistakes of the young person transitioning into adulthood!

## *Invite The Teenager's Opinions And Input When Appropriate*

A third suggestion suggests that parents look for opportunities for teens to give their opinions and make up their own minds. This task is difficult for parents because they have been making decisions for their children from birth. Many parents even try to prevent their children from making some of the same mistakes they made growing up; these parents stifle their adolescent's development by being overly protective. Some parents help their son or daughter on several homework projects, which enables the young person to get a better grade. Perhaps, their help would be needed less if they had been more willing to allow him or her to suffer once or twice when lack of planning caused the natural consequence of failure. As a concerned parent, they could have still been available to help when asked, but careful not to "rescue" them which leads to dependency and quite likely decreases the opportunity of learning from such a mistake.

## *Be Optimistic—This Demonstrates A Positive Outlook*

Fourth, parents need to demonstrate a positive outlook or be optimistic about this period of their son or daughter's development. Parents would do better if they learned to ignore some things— perhaps many things that if left alone will take care of themselves. Parents must guard against exaggerating the difficulties they face on the home front. I get angry when I hear some parents talk about the misery they are experiencing because of their teenagers. From their descriptions, one would only assume they are talking about beasts of the lowest form—not a person created in the image of God and perhaps in many ways merely a product of their parental teaching and upbringing.

If parents adopt the philosophy that problems are opportunities, this period of development will go much smoother than if they choose to harp on every challenge or disagreement they have with their son or daughter. Some have said that "attitude is everything!" Perhaps it isn't everything, but it does contribute significantly to how difficult or manageable a challenge becomes. If a dad or mom approaches a potential problem as an opportunity to teach or clarify a value, explaining the purpose and reason behind the value, they will be less apt to over-react and thus create alienation between their teenager and themselves.

## *Begin Communication With Your Children*

Suggestion five encourages parents to begin communication with their children—even if they have had none for several months. One hopes that parents would have established some good communication patterns, but if not, they must begin. It is never too late to change! In a news story printed in *The Columbus Dispatch*, Julia Osborne summarized what several professionals working with adolescents prioritized as important principles for communication with teenagers (1). Parents are encouraged to:

- **Listen** *but not tell them how to deal with things*

- **Talk to them** *on their time, not only when it's convenient for the parent*

- **Talk to them privately**

- **Watch their tone of voice** *and body language*

- **Acknowledge the child's feelings** *by showing respect for attitudes*

- **Express feelings** *about their behavior without attacking it or them*

- **Ask for explanations**, *or what happened rather than why*

- **Ask** *for more* **details**

- **Avoid telling** *too many anecdotes*

- **Pick their battles**, *but be willing to compromise when appropriate*

- **Avoid using absolutes**

- *Work on* **solving problems together**

- **Remember** *that their children are growing up*

- **Provide positive, constructive comments** *when possible*

- **Coordinate a united front** *as parents by being consistent*

- **Be patient** *and "hang in there"*

- **Seek advice** *when necessary or when it can be helpful*

## *Focus On The Relationship And Strive To Be A Good Friend*

Sixth (and closely associated with the fifth), parents should focus on the relationship and strive to be a good friend to their teenager by taking on the characteristics of a good friend. A friend does not condemn, criticize, or ostracize. A friend cautions when someone is headed toward danger but in a caring, supportive manner that makes the message more acceptable. A friend likewise takes an interest in the things that are important to that individual. A friend gives the gift of understanding and is slow to judge (2).

Being a friend takes time. As a parent, I might not be at all interested in Saturday afternoon wrestling, but can enhance my father-son relationship immensely if I take the time to view it with my son. Saturday morning cartoons can become quite tolerable if one approaches this activity as an opportunity to spend quality time with their preschooler. Most parents will find it hard to understand the latest fashion in dress, hairstyles, and totally lack appreciation for contemporary music, but they can work on accepting the importance it may have for their daughter if they are to become her true friend. At the very least parents can try to understand it by showing some effort and some respect for that child's opinions and interests.

## *Parents Must Model What They Would Like To See In Their Teenager*

Lastly, and perhaps most important of all, parents must model what they would like to see in their teenager's behavior and attitude. "Actions speak louder than words" is not just an old cliché but is a practice that has significant application in this stage of parenting. This practice is important and works well at all levels of childhood but perhaps best during adolescence. During this period of parenting, the parents' influence is almost nil compared to all the other forces that compete for the teenager's attention and focus. If teenagers will not listen to their parents, at least their parents can show them through their modeling what they would like to see them become. The majority of studies in human development confirm that adolescents tend to reclaim the value system of their parents after they get through this period of questioning and sometimes rebelliousness. Most parents would be better off if they talked less and acted more. This is why, in many of his writings, James Dobson refers to the importance of modeling since more things are "caught than taught" all through childhood.

## *Parent-Teenager Communication*

An article once appeared in *Possibilities* by Robert Schuller Ministries that focused on teenage rebellion and alcoholism. A follow-up to this article focused on parent-teenager communication. **Parents are encouraged to consider the following principles in talking with their teenagers** (3):

### *Put Yourself In Their Shoes*

Do you remember how you felt when you were thirteen, fifteen, or seventeen? If you were like most teenagers, you probably worried excessively about what your peers thought of you. Sometimes you felt awkward and unattractive. You fluctuated between feeling grown up and hopelessly childish. But you survived, and your teens will, too. By remembering what it was like, you can be a more understanding parent.

### *Listen*

The majority of teens complain that parents do not really hear them when they speak. Active listening allows you to focus on the other person's feelings and send back a message of empathetic understanding. You do not need to evaluate, offer advice, analyze, or ask a lot of questions. Understand their true concerns first before responding.

### *Use Words That Build up, Not Tear Down*

Your teen needs your encouragement more than you might think. Discouraging words such as "You never do it right!" or "You're always late!" tend to kill self-esteem. If a conversation starts to heat up, take a time out before sarcastic, cutting words slip out.

### *Be Honest*

Let your teen see you as the imperfect, but growing, human that you are. You do not have to have all the answers to maintain their respect. Share with them how you worry about being a good parent and sometimes do not know how to handle the problems that come up. Most important, admit when you have been wrong.

### *Be Patient And Pray*

Remember, God knows what it's like to be a parent. He wants the best for you and your teenager. Talk to God often about your concerns and encourage your teenage son or daughter to do likewise. Allow God to become an invisible, loving member of your family.

**Teenagers are encouraged to consider the following principles in talking to their parents (4):**

### *Put Yourself In Their Shoes*

They may not want to admit it, but your parents sometimes feel inadequate as leaders in your family. It is especially unnerving for them to see their "little" boy or girl suddenly growing up. They worry that they have not done enough to teach good values. Understanding how your parents feel may help you be more sensitive to their concerns.

### *Try Not To Retreat*

Many parents complain that their teenagers never talk to them anymore. The closeness they once experienced is replaced with stony silences. Often they do not understand your need for privacy and independence, or how it hurts you when they pretend to hear you but are not really listening. Tell your parents the kind of things that make you want to clam up. And listen to their concerns, too.

### *Use Words That Communicate Respect*

If you are like most teenagers, you do not like some of the restrictions your parents have placed upon you. You may not understand their reasons for the rules. Try to talk openly and calmly with your parents about what bothers you. Use "I" messages: "I know that this is important to you, but it makes me feel you do not trust me. Help me understand your reasoning." If a conversation begins to deteriorate into an angry exchange, take a time out and resume the talk later or write out your feelings in a note and present it to your parent with the request to talk further.

### *Be Honest*

It is difficult to tell the whole truth if you are worried about your parents' reactions. But remember that they were your age once, too, and probably understand your problems better than you think. Give them a chance to help you by keeping the communication lines open.

### *Be Patient And Pray*

God is not finished with you—or your parents—yet! All of you have more growing to do. Allow God to be your heavenly parent, the one you turn to for guidance on how you relate to your earthly parents.

# Chapter 11

# Approaching Special Challenges

※

*When pride comes, then comes disgrace,*
*but with humility comes wisdom.*
*Proverbs 11:2*

Although the concepts presented in this book apply to all parenting situations, there are many factors that can disrupt the usual course of parenting, requiring unique skills and expanded understanding to meet the challenge. While divorce will severely impact many homes and thus alter normal parenting styles, there are many other factors that can cause disruption in the course of parenting. Some homes with both parents present can be as dysfunctional as ones resulting from a catastrophe or some other major trauma in the family network. Christians are not exempt from problems; all too often families within the church will be faced with challenging stressors. **Divorce,** or **premature death of a spouse** sometimes leaves one parent to raise children; if **single parents choose to remarry,** they are faced with the challenge of **reconstituting the family,** and the role of **step-parenting** comes into play. **"Blending" two separate family systems** into a new one can be extremely challenging and tax the resources of both the parent and step-parent. Experts in the field of child development and family systems report that such a transition could take up to 5 years.

Christian couples who **suffer from infertility** may consider opening their homes and hearts to a needy child, choosing to become **adoptive parents**. Although adoption of an infant child may not pose any greater challenge than having natural children, many adoptions involve children beyond infancy and ones that have multiple needs. **Foster parenting a needy child** on a temporary basis is a special ministry for families that have the resources and commitment required to handle such situations successfully. As the number of children needing foster care surges, the pool of good homes available appears inadequate to meet the demand. Foster parenting can be a wonderful experience and beautiful ministry opportunity for the family that is equipped with the necessary resources.

To understand the implications of such specialized parental roles, let us first turn our attention to some of the characteristics that cause dysfunction within the family unit. According to Peter Gerlock, there are several **characteristics that seem to prevail in dysfunctional families** (1). This does not imply that all such features will be present in any home experiencing trouble, or that families in transition from some form of trauma will become dysfunctional. Some families face adversity and transition through catastrophe without serious problems. However, if the trauma causes significant disruption and no efforts to stabilize the family system are made, the family becomes vulnerable to a dysfunctional and ultimately destructive process.

## Symptoms Of Dysfunction Within Families

**Dysfunctional families seem to reproduce themselves**. Poor habits, attitudes, and teaching that prevail in such families usually have a history going back to previous generations, and these **"customs" seem to be inherited from one generation to the next**. Although help is often available to these families, they tend to be **closed to resources or ideas outside the family.**

**Family secrets often exist**, but they are **well-defended through denial and projection of blame onto others outside the family**, including institutions such as church, school, and community agencies or other family-related organizations. Such secrets can range from unfaithfulness of the parents to drug abuse and alcoholism.

Other family secrets may include physical or sexual abuse of one or more of its members or some other acting out behavior that is well hidden by the family.

Although members of all families have some degree of emotional expression, dysfunctional family members **often exhibit more dramatic or greater emotional expression** than those from non-dysfunctional families. They may experience **an excess of certain emotions such as fear, shame, and guilt. Inconsistent humor — too little humor or hurtful forms of humor** — can be characteristic in these families. Frequently such families **have rigid or inconsistent rules. Role reversal between members** of the family, especially in the parent-child roles, is common. This phenomenon can include grandparents if the extended family members are an active part of the dysfunction within the family. Instead of a buffer to protect children from outside stressors, parents become stressors to their children. Instead of teaching, protecting, modeling, and encouraging growth in a positive manner, **parents give messages to their offspring that convey rejection and neglect** in meeting the child's needs and fulfilling the parental role.

The list of parental messages in dysfunctional homes, either stated or perceived, often includes the following: "Don't trust"... "Don't talk"..."I love you, but go away"... "You're wonderful... you're worthless"..."You're responsible for our family problems"... "I'll love you if..." Despite the powerlessness children feel, such messages leave **children to internalize blame for their family's dysfunction and unhappiness**. As a result of such messages, children experience shame, guilt, hurt, and anger. **The message that "feelings are not okay" seems to predominate** at all levels in the dysfunctional family.

**Physical, emotional, and sexual abuse are often associated with such homes.** The dynamics of such families vacillate between the extremes of **enmeshment, where all members are too closely entangled with each other without sufficient boundaries,** to the opposite extreme of **disengagement, where all members of the family operate independently and show no investment in or support of each other.**

# Six Tasks For Child Recoving From Divorce Or Loss

With divorce, children experience what Judith Wallerstein describes as an extended period of disequilibrium, which may last several years or longer (2). Based on a ten-year study of divorcing families, Wallerstein reports that the adjustments required for the child following a divorce or bereavement in losing a parent will stretch over several years of childhood and adolescence. According to this research, which is highly regarded within the child develop-ment field, the child will need to accomplish six (6) major tasks to successfully survive the effects of such a loss.

## *Acknowledge the reality of the marital rupture*

The first task for the recovering child in a divorce of his parents is to acknowledge the reality of the marital rupture. Most children, like adults, tend to deny that the family unit they have known is disrupting or changing radically. Such a change is usually not desired by the children, nor have they had any input, making acceptance a bigger challenge. Most children of divorce continue for years to have the fantasy that their birth parents will get back together and that all of them can live happily ever after. This fantasy, along with fears of parental abandonment, disaster, being overwhelmed by feelings of sorrow, anger, and rejection, and a yearning for keeping things the way they were further hamper the task of acknowledgement.

Much like a child who has lost a parent from death, the child of divorce fears losing the other parent and being left alone; that fear is so strong that it may keep the child from resolving this task for some time. Through adult support and mutual parenting of the child by both parents, the child can master this task in about one year from the separation.

Family therapy experts tell us that children of divorce struggle with loyalty issues; they want to be loyal to both mother and father, but feel they can only be loyal to the one they are with. Since mom and dad no longer love each other, they feel they can't despite their compelling desire to love both. When with their father, the child feels he must be loyal to dad and disloyal to mom. When with mom, the opposite is true. Divorced parents must help their children from falling into this confusion which therapists call "mixed loyalty conflict." Parents **must encourage an ongoing relationship with the opposite parent, admonish against any display of disrespect for either parent, and advised that they don't have to take sides.** These children need reassurance that despite mom and dad no longer loving each other, that they can still love both mom and dad and that both parents will continue to love them just as before.

## *Disengage From Parental Conflict & Distress Begin Resuming Customary Pursuits*

The second major task for the child of divorced parents is what Wallerstein calls disengaging from parental conflict and distress and resuming customary pursuits (school, play, and relationships), which can take up to one-and-one-half years following the separation. As difficult as it may seem for parents who are still very angry at each other for the things that may have caused the divorce, they need to help their children see their difficulties as a parental issue and not allow children to personalize blame. Quite often parents continue to keep their children in the middle of the conflict rather than allowing them to deal with their own feelings about the trauma they have experienced. Once children are given opportunities to acknowledge and handle their own feelings of anxiety, depression, and loss, they can resolve such feelings and turn attention back to school, peer relationships and other normal childhood issues.

Divorced parents may not have anything in common except their children, but it is most important that they communicate and provide some consistency in conveying their continued love and support for the children. **Instead of spousal parents who are married, they may need to become "professional" parents** who are no longer in love or married. Parenting may need to take on the context of a job with a **cooperative attitude** and **respect between co-workers.** People can learn to work with someone they don't love. Out of respect for each other as persons, they learn to cooperate as co-workers and produce a common product or work toward the same goal. In the case of divorced parents, the product is their children and the goal is helping them attain adulthood successfully.

Divorced parents have divorced each other, but have not divorced themselves from the children or their responsibility to complete parenting. **The better they communicate and coordinate efforts, the better chance of producing a successful outcome; the worse they accomplish these tasks, the greater the likelihood of dysfunction.**

## *Resolve The Loss*

The third task children of divorce must accomplish has to do with resolving the loss they feel in the disruption of their family. According to Wallerstein's research, this task may be one of the most difficult ones, and it may take several years to establish a good relationship with a future step-parent. **Children must overcome a sense of rejection, lovelessness, powerlessness, responsibility or blame for the loss of family, and other such self-defeating feelings.** This task is accomplished by establishing a **reliable visiting pattern** and **ongoing communication** with the parent with whom the child no longer lives. Continually reminding the child of his or her parents' love and the child's blamelessness in the divorce is an absolute must to reassure the child and help him or her reach resolution of this task. Family therapy sessions including both birth parents and step-parents are often necessary during this stage to assist the family in giving the child this message and to work out consistent visiting plans and other arrangements.

## *Resolve Anger & Self-Blame*

Resolving anger, self-blame and other strong emotional responses becomes the fourth major task for children of divorce. **Children generally always seem to blame someone—** mother, father, or more than likely in divorce situations, themselves. Children have often told me in therapy sessions that they feel if they had gotten better grades, always kept their rooms clean, obeyed their parents better, or hadn't argued with their younger brother or sister, that their parents wouldn't have divorced. While I try to assure them that these are all good things to do, these are not the things that cause divorce. Divorce is an adult decision; they neither caused the divorce nor could they have prevented it. Perhaps the terrible thing about divorce for children is that it is a major decision that dramatically affects their lives; despite having no input, they are just forced to accept it and deal with the consequences that it brings.

Quite often **after blame surfaces, anger follows**. In some situations, anger can be long-standing and intense, especially among older children and adolescents. The goal of this task is to assist children in achieving some perspective regarding the reasons that prompted the divorce as well as understanding that both parents continue to care for and love them as they always did. As with the third task, ongoing reassurance regarding the child's lack of blame or guilt in the divorce and redefining it as an adult issue that really had nothing to do with the children may be helpful. Depending on the level of conflict and maturity of the family members working through this task, it may take as long as five to ten years to accomplish successfully and may require outside professional help through family therapy or counseling.

## *Accept the Permanence Or Finality Of Divorce*

A fifth task for the child traumatized by divorce involves accepting the permanence or finality of divorce. Such acceptance may take the child years to accept, even when a parent remarries. Almost all children fantasize that their parents will eventually get back together so their family would be the way it is suppose to be. I have had children tell me that if they pray enough, they are confident that God will answer their prayers and bring mom and dad back together again. For the most part, this is unrealistic and to allow the child to believe this will cause much confusion and frustration when his or her faith doesn't bring about the results he has prayed and hoped would be accomplished.

Here it is important to help the child come to understand that God hears his or her prayers; but, that God will not force his mother or father to do something against their will. In some cases, since the trust has been so completely damaged with the things that led to the divorce, rebuilding trust would quite likely be next to impossible. Perhaps this is why God permits divorce as a result of what most churches accept as "Biblical grounds" for divorce. However, the child probably will not understand such concepts and to attempt explaining these would only lead to further confusion and more intense emotions.

Rather than trying to explain these "adult" concepts to a child, our efforts would produce better benefits by helping the child learn more about God's grace. Perhaps by **explaining that God gives "grace" as the added strength we need during times of trouble will help the child better direct his prayers and lead to less frustration and anger when his prayers are not answered in the way he or she desires.**

## *Achieve A Realistic Hope Regarding Relationships*

Lastly, Wallerstein says a child will need to achieve a realistic hope regarding relationships. Having survived the loss of a desirable relationship or having been challenged to accept redefinitions of their families as a result of the divorce, children will need to resolve their feelings regarding it to have optimism regarding their future relationships, especially as adults. Continued focus on the children's needs and interest by both parents as well as reassurance of their love can be a great asset in helping children through this task successfully as well as the earlier ones listed.

Perhaps one of the most important aspects in resolution is to see that the parental figures involved likewise model resolution of the past conflict. Child development researchers report that **children seem to adapt to things, even traumas like divorce, in about the same manner that they see the adults in their lives adapt to the trauma.** If children see parents modeling forgiveness and resolution of the conflicts that led to the divorce, then children will be more apt to "move on" and likewise practice forgiveness. Should the adults continue to harbor resentments and resist forgiveness, perhaps even subtly exhibit hostility, resentment, and even bitterness, then these factors will likely prevent the child from putting these conflicts aside and gaining this hope for future relationships.

## *Surviving Other Issues Resulting From Divorce Or Loss*

There are a multitude of other issues for children who experience divorce and will for at least part of their childhood live in a single-parent home. Peter Gerlock says that such children encounter many changes in their lives (3). They will **need to survive the disbelief, shock, guilt, self-doubt, fear, hurt, rage, blame, shame, and depression** that often follow the announcement of divorce or separation by their parents. Following such a shock, comes the reality of having less time with parents and being alone more. Not only will they see the non-custodial parent less, but they will also see less of the custodial parent as he or she performs additional tasks in the absence of the other parent.

**Children are quite often given parental status,** which Gerlock calls **parentification** in hopes that they will take on more responsibility (4). This is certainly not conducive to helping the child deal with the divorce. Some single parents even try putting their adolescent or pre-adolescent sons or daughters in a more adult role in an effort to encourage more independence and responsibility. In addition to all these changes in the young person's life, he or she is also **faced with a redefinition of roles and rules with grandparents, siblings, and peers.** Do the children continue to have the same kind of relationship with grandparents and see them as frequently as they did prior to the divorce? Are visits to the non-custodial grandparents cut off? Do older children have to take on babysitting roles for younger children in the family, severely limiting their ability to participate in peer, social, or school activities? All these and other questions are ones that face children and families experiencing divorce.

Divorce often **disrupts the physical environment**; larger homes must be sold to meet a reduced budget and family size. Such changes can also cause **changes in school placement**, which may have adverse effects on children's motivation, performance, and overall school adjustment. Amid all these changes, children probably

**fear further loss**; prior security is lost to **feelings of hopelessness and powerlessness** about what is happening in their lives. Although very important to helping children get through the trauma of divorce successfully, grieving is often postponed or put off in hopes that their dreams of parental reconciliation will somehow come true.

If children are successful in getting through the various tasks related to divorce, chances are good that their lives will change once again because of the remarriage of biological parents. A child has probably just begun feeling less anxious and angry as he or she begins accepting the new situation as "okay" when once again the challenge of change is thrust upon the child. In most cases, the child is challenged to deal with the prospect of a step-parent much too soon after the divorce of his parents and prior to accomplishing the developmental tasks that help resolve the divorce issue for the child.

While trying to "finish up" the divorce, the family takes on a new relationship with a step-parent. Loyalty conflicts surface almost immediately. The children will wonder what to call the new step-parent—by his or her first name, or "Dad" or "Mom." If they refer to the step-parent as dad or mom, does that mean they feel their natural parent is less significant with the step-parent in the picture? There may be a **different set of rules and expectations, roles will change**, and sometimes **the biological parent pressures children toward complete acceptance of and loyalty to the new step-parent**. Other times, the new step-parent, in exuberance, tries to take on too much leadership in the family and especially in discipline of his or her step-children. Most research studies available on step-parenting **recommend that the step-parent progress quite slowly in taking an active role in discipline of step-children, leaving the major parental tasks to the natural parent and putting all his or her efforts toward building a good relationship** with step-children based on love, care, acceptance, and appreciation. Both step-parents and step-children need time to get to know each other and develop this relationship. A step-parent thus faces not only the usual experiences of child rearing but also problems and feelings resulting from a major upset in his life (5).

## *Changes Facing Step-Children*

As with divorce, there are several developmental tasks that step-children need to go through to deal with changes successfully. First, they must grieve multiple losses. As already mentioned, many children continue to hold onto the fantasy that their divorced parents will get back together, despite indications to the contrary. When one or the other parent remarries, the child comes one step closer toward the realization that such a dream probably will not occur. Upon considering such a reality, the guilt and self-doubt that followed the divorce may resurface and need to be resolved again. While trying once again to resolve the loss involved in the divorce and the accompanying emotions, children must redefine **the question of "Who is my family?" Discipline, diet, division of labor, and turf issues all create problems** that are not easy, but are nonetheless manageable if family members learn to cooperate (6).

## *Foster & Adoptive Home Placements*

**Foster homes** are intended for temporary placement of children who should eventually return to their biological families. These **temporary homes often provide for youngsters whose families are in crisis or who need protective services** to prevent abuse and neglect. **Adoption is a permanent commitment to the adoptive child**; the rights and responsibilities of the biological parents are terminated and legally transferred to the adoptive parents. Adoption has made marvelously happy family lives possible for many childless people, and it may answer questions or doubts some people experience about having children (7).

A great number of children are made available for adoption, either surrendered voluntarily by parents or permanently removed from their homes for their safety and protection because they have been abused or severely neglected and the parents' rights to parent them are terminated by the Courts. For children who come from such homes, only specialized environments with available resources and therapies should be considered for placement. Such children have often experienced more than one divorce, several step-parents, and more than one foster or adoptive home placement. Some such children may have even spent time in a hospital or residential treatment center. A specialized treatment setting designed to help children who suffer such traumas can successfully treat such children and prepare them to return to their families or another family setting—either foster or adoptive homes. For Christian individuals or couples who wish to take on this opportunity for ministry, further training and a greater awareness of related issues will be absolutely necessary for success in working with such a child. Such parenting situations will probably require support from a professional therapist to assist with the child's ongoing adjustment and development.

# Chapter 12

# Christian Parenting—
# A Reasonable Challenge!

※

*For nothing is impossible with God.*
*Luke 1:37*

*I can do everything through him who gives me strength.*
*Philippians 4:13*

Despite the commitment we have to our children and the challenge that we may feel as Christian parents, there are still those times that discouragement sets in. Perhaps the following prayer (1) should become our model and philosophy to follow in the parenting of our children (and for those of us at this later stage in life, grandparenting of our grandchildren).

### Oh God, Make Me A Better Parent

**Help me to understand my children, to listen patiently to what they have to say and to answer all their questions kindly. Keep me from interrupting them, talking back to them and contradicting them. Make me as courteous to them as I would have them be to me. Give me the courage to confess my sins against**

my children and to ask of them forgiveness, when I know that I have done them wrong.

May I not vainly hurt the feelings of my children. Forbid that I should laugh at their mistakes or resort to shame and ridicule as punishment. Let me not tempt a child to lie and steal. So guide me hour by hour that I may demonstrate by all I say and do that honesty produces happiness.

Reduce, I pray, the meaness in me. May I cease to nag; and when I am out of sorts, help me, Oh Lord, to hold my tongue. Blind me to the little errors of my children and help me to see the good things that they do. Give me a ready word for honest praise.

Help me to treat my children as those of their own age, but let me not exact of them the judgments and conventions of adults. Allow me not to rob them of the opportunity to wait upon themselves, to think, to choose, and to make decisions.

Forbid that I should ever punish them for my selfish satisfaction. May I grant them all of their wishes that are reasonable and have the courage always to withhold a privilege which I know will do them harm.

Make me so fair and just, so considerate and companionable to my children that they will have a genuine esteem for me. Fit me to be loved and imitated by my children. With all thy gifts, Oh God, do give me calm and poise and self-control.

Gary C. Myers
Co-Founder and Editor
Highlights For Children
Copyright by Highlights for Children, Inc., Columbus, OH
1884—1971

Is successful Christian parenting possible—even in today's world? Yes! Absolutely yes! With God's help, anyone can succeed as a Christian parent despite the challenges today's world provides. Greater is He that is within me than he that is in the world!

# Endnotes

**Chapter 1**
**Is Christian Parenting Even Possible In Today's World?**

**Chapter 2**
**The Importance Of A Good Parent-Child Relationship**

1. Dahms, William. "Authority vs. Relationship." *Child Care Quarterly*. 7 (4). Winter, 1978, 3-9.
2. Ibid., p 3.
3. Zigler, Zig. "Positive Steps to Developing Positive Kids," *Possibilities*. Summer, 1986, p. 23.
4. Ibid., p. 23.

**Chapter 3**
**Developing Good Communication With Your Child**

1. Gordan, Thomas. *Parent Effectiveness Training*. New York: Peter H. Wyden, Inc., 1972, pp. 40—44.
2. Ibid., p. 58.
3. Ibid., pp. 109-110.
4. Ibid., p. 111.
5. Ibid., p. 113.
6. Ibid., p. 114.
7. Ibid., p. 52.

## Chapter 4
## Communicating To Help Solve Problems

1. Gordan, Thomas. *Parent Effectiveness Training*. New York: Peter H. Wyden, Inc., 1972, pp. 40-44.
2. Ibid., pp. 52-53.
3. Ibid., pp. 15-16.
4. Ibid., p. 65.
5. Ibid., pp. 66-67.
6. Ibid., pp. 67-68.
7. Ibid., p. 115.
8. Ibid., pp. 116-117.
9. Ibid., pp. 115-116.

## Chapter 5
## Understanding Your Children

1. Gessell Institute, Ames and Rodell. *Infant and Child in the Culture Today*. NewYork: Harper & Row, 1943.
Gessell Institute and Ames. *The Child From Five To Ten*. New York: Harper & Row, 1946.
Gessell Institute. Youth: *The Years From Ten To Sixteen*. New York: Harper & Row, 1956.

## Chapter 6
## Parents Must Be A Team!

1. Norton, R. G. *Parenting*. New Jersey: Prentice-Hall, Inc., 1972, p. 45.
2. Ibid., p. 141.

## Chapter 7
## Understanding Punishment And Discipline

1. Keating, Kathleen. *The Hug Therapy Book*. Minneapolis: CompCare Publishers, 1983.

2. May, Gary. *Child Discipline Guidelines For Parents.* National Committee For Prevention of Child Abuse, 1986, p. 4.
3. Ibid., p. 4.
4. Ibid., p. 4.
5. Ibid., p. 4.
6. Krumboltz, J.D. and H.D., *Changing Children's Behavior.* Englewood Cliffs: Prentice-Hall, Inc., 1972, p. 78.
7. May, p. 4.
8. Maurer, A., and Wallerstein, J., "The Bible and the Rod," Berkley: The Committee To End Violence Against the Next Generation, 1982, p. 4.
9. Funk & Wagnalls Standard Desk Dictionary. New York: Harper & Row, 1984, p. 220.
10. Valusek, John E. "People Are Not For Hitting," Unpublished. (Used With Permission).
11. Ibid.
12. Ibid.

## Chapter 8
## Teaching Right From Wrong With Good Discipline

1. Morris, Richard. *Behavior Modification With Children: A Systematic Guide.* Cambridge: Winthrop Publishers, Inc., 1976, p. 45.
2. Miller, David E. *The Stop...Think...Do...Program: A Workbook For Children With ADD or ADHD.* USA: Xulon Press, Inc., 2004.
3. Blackwood, R. *Operant Control of Behavior.* Akron: Exordum Press, 1971, p. 13.
4. Lerman, Saf. *Parent Awareness Training.* New York: A & W Publishers, Inc., pp. 222-225.

## Chapter 9
## Sticking To Essentials

## Chapter 10
## Remaining Patient During Adolescence

1. Osborne, Julie. "How To Talk To Your Teenager." *The Columbus Dispatch*. October 4, 1987, Section C, p. 1. (Used With Permission)
2. McKee, Michael. *Questions And Answers About Teenagers*. Columbus: Ohio Psychology Publishing Co., 1984, p. 3.
3. Crystal Cathedral Ministries. "How To Talk To Your Teen—How To Talk To Your Parents." *Possibilities*. Garden Grove: Robert Schuller Ministries, Jan-Feb, 1987, p. 8.
4. Ibid., p. 8.

## Chapter 11
## Approaching Special Challenges

1. Gerlock, Peter. Workshop sponsored by Step-family Association of Illinois, Inc. (National Association of Homes For Children Conference), 1987.
2. Wallerstein, J. "Psychological Tasks For Children of Divorce," *American Journal of Ortho-Psychiatry*. 53, 2, April, 1983, p. 235.
3. Gerlock.
4. Gerlock.
5. Hendricks, Howard (Ed.). "Stepparents." *The Encyclopedia of Christian Parenting*. Old Tappan: Fleming H. Revel Company, 1982, p. 409.
6. Bohannon, Paul, and Erickson, Rosemary. "Stepping In," *Psychology Today*. February, 1978, p. 56.
7. Hendrick, Adoption, p. 29.

## Chapter 12
## Christian Parenting—A Reasonable Challenge!

1. Meyers, Gary. "A Parent's Prayer," *Highlights For Children, Inc.* Columbus, OH.

LaVergne, TN USA
16 June 2010
186286LV00003B/33/A